SECURITY, CULTURE AND HUMAN RIGHTS IN THE MIDDLE EAST AND SOUTH ASIA

SECURITY, CULTURE AND HUMAN RIGHTS IN THE MIDDLE EAST AND SOUTH ASIA

CHRISTOPH BLUTH

Global Research Publications
2019

To order additional copies of this book, contact:
Xlibris
800-056-3182
www.Xlibrispublishing.co.uk
Orders@Xlibrispublishing.co.uk
801340

CONTENTS

PART I
Pakistan

PART II
Iraq

PART III
Iran

CHAPTER 1

Introduction

In the last five years, Europe has confronted a major refugee crisis which has multiple causes, including major violent conflict in the Middle East and Africa, as well as drought and poverty, all of which have been linked to man-made global warming as well as complex political mechanisms.

The large-scale migration of people to Europe has had significant political consequences in the countries who are members of the European Union in particular. In 2015 alone a total of about 1.3 million people sought protection in the European Union. A report from the CSIS described the impact in the following terms: "Many European nations have incurred significant costs from migration movements. A small nation of 9.5 million, Sweden is expected to have taken in a number of refugees totalling nearly two percent of its population, more acceptances per capita than any other European nation. The fiscal cost of asylum seekers reached 1.0 percent of Sweden's Gross Domestic Product (GDP) in 2016. In the same year, Denmark spent 0.57 percent of its GDP, and Germany spent 0.35 percent of its GDP on asylum seekers. It is generally understood that this level of displacement has had a profound and unprecedented level of impact in the humanitarian, security, and economic spaces in Europe."[1]

Unless governments make other arrangements, or refugees qualify for immigration under the various rules that apply to skilled labour or other such categories, refugees are admitted under procedures for claiming asylum. The right to asylum is a an ancient concept according to which a person may be protected by some sovereign authority, nowadays normally the government of another country, The concept of asylum and right to grant such protection was recognized by the ancient Egyptians, Greeks and Hebrews and evolved to the concept of asylum (sometimes referred to as political asylum) in the Western tradition which has now be codified in international conventions and the domestic law of countries who have acceded to the conventions.

The United Nations Universal Declaration of Human Rights of 1948 stated that "everyone has the right to seek and to enjoy in other countries asylum from persecution". This principle was codified further in the 1951 Convention Relating to the Status of Refugees and the Protocol Relating to the Status of Refugees 1967. A refugee is defined as a person who is located outside the country of which he or she is a national due to fear of persecution on certain grounds, such as race, nationality, religion, political opinions or membership of a particular social group or participation in certain social activities. In the European Union, the right to asylum is also provided for by Article 8 of the European Convention on Human Rights which protects the right to a private and family life.

The United Kingdom has introduced a complex range of legislation to codify its adherence to the international conventions including the ECHR. These include the Immigration Act 1971, Immigration and Asylum Act 1999, Nationality Immigration and Asylum Act 2002, Asylum and Immigration (Treatment of Claimants etc.) Act 2004, Borders Citizenship and Immigration Act 2009, Immigration Act 2014 and Immigration Act 2016.

An assessment of an asylum application involves extensive interviews, often conducted with the aid of an interpreter, other evidence submitted by the applicant including testimonials, copies of arrest warrants or similar documents to prove persecution in their own country, and submissions from the solicitor if the applicant is represented.

The large majority of asylum applications are refused by the Home Office. Whereas in the 1980s around 20% of asylum applications were refused in the first stage, this figure rose substantially by 2004 to almost 90% and has remained very high ever since. In recent years it has fluctuated around a level of 75%. In 2018 38% of the refusals were overturned by tribunals on appeal.

This study is not concerned with the asylum policy of the United Kingdom per se but reviewing tribunal judgements and the appropriate literature provides some understanding of the factors that drive asylum policy as it is implemented by the UK Home Office. Any notion that official policy is based with any concern to provide protection for persons in need of it dies with the first encounter of how asylum applicants are dealt with in practice. The central objective of government policy with respect to asylum seekers is to find by any means possible a path to deny protection without violating the government's obligation with respect to the conventions that it has signed on to. Asylum is only granted if officials are absolutely certain that they would lose on appeal, and they are willing to take substantial risks in this respect. There is little evidence of any concern for the enormous litany of human tragedy that officials encounter on a daily basis.

It is important to note that this conduct is not unique to the authorities of the United Kingdom. In other European countries the behaviour of immigration authorities charged with dealing with asylum applications is quite similar. It is even worse in Australia and the United States government under President Trump is striving to reduce the admission of refugees to zero, although it is thwarted by the judiciary. The fact that asylum applications are dealt with by the same authorities responsible for all immigration matters, as is universally the case in Western countries, is indicative of how it is viewed. Asylum is not primarily about immigration, but about providing protection against persecution. But the fact that it is dealt with by the immigration authorities means that it becomes subject to the priorities of immigration policy which is to limit the influx of people in need and maximize the opportunities for wealthy or highly educated and skilled individuals.

The paradox that the goals of asylum policy and immigration policy are in conflict but are dealt with by the same bureaucratic institutions has been noted in a study in the International Journal of

Refugee Studies: "The institution of asylum faces a serious crisis in Europe. At the root of this problem lies the perception that refugee law and asylum practice obstruct the efficient enforcement of a restrictive immigration policy. It is also seen to weaken the deterrence effect of the main instruments (punishment, forcible expulsion) used to combat unwanted immigration. This crisis highlights the need to explain the following question: Why should asylum be granted, given that EU Member States are committed to a restrictive immigration regime. Past explanations of the purpose of asylum are not fully satisfactory on this account. ...The human rights theory is capable of explaining asylum practice against the background of a restrictive immigration regime, but relies exclusively on altruism. Also, the proliferation of human rights results in the plea for asylum for all human rights victims conflicting with a restrictive immigration policy. If the human rights theory were taken seriously, States would find it difficult to realise the policy goal of restricting immigration."[2]

There are two issues that in most cases are critical for the outcome of an asylum case – the general credibility of applicants and the background information about the country of origin. This study is concerned with the latter. It provides a guide to some of the key issues of asylum cases involving refugees from South Asia and the Middle East.

The study of how the UK authorities deal with asylum applications yields some surprising insights. The first is how extraordinarily poor the country information is that the authorities have at their disposal. The Home Office publishes Country Information and Guidance notes which based on an eclectic selection of (paradoxically) reports from human rights organisations, the UNHCR and various newspaper reports. Although the names of the authors of the Guidance Notes are not revealed, it is clear that they are not experts in the field and do not make systematic use of academic research. Compared to the actual refusal documents issued to applicants however they are a paragon of objectivity. Although the government has through the Foreign Office, the intelligence agencies and external advisers a very substantial information gathering capability, it appears that none of that is used to provide the Home Office with country evidence in relation to asylum cases which has to rely on Wikipedia and other dubious internet sources. Just to cite one example in which the use of information from intelligence services might be useful would relates to the question as to whether the Vietnamese authorities use their intelligence capabilities in the United Kingdom to track dissenters and to film and analyse protests outside the embassy. It is known that in Vietnam the filming of protests with the use of facial recognition software is standard practice. Moreover, Vietnamese citizens in the United Kingdom regularly report that Vietnamese agents infiltrate the diaspora and are aware of all Vietnamese citizens and their activities. Using information derived from intelligence at a tribunal might be problematic but it could be factored into the initial assessment without being even referred to. However, in this case every Vietnamese political activist in the United Kingdom might have to be given asylum. Thus, the UK authorities maintain that there is "no proof" that the Vietnamese authorities monitor their own citizens in the United Kingdom. This puts the UK authorities into the position of having to maintain the stance that they have no evidence of what is actually a threat to the national security of the country.

The tactics used by the authorities are quite transparent. If the statements by the applicant are not supported by external evidence of any kind, then they are rejected for this reason. If there is objective evidence that supports the statements by the applicants, the authorities claim that the applicant could had discovered this information by using publicly available sources and therefore it proves nothing.

However, it is very common for officials to get their facts wrong. They use dubious sources, or they do not understand the context of the information they are using. They treat a country's legislation as if it defined actual policy, without considering the implementation of the legislation or the actual behaviour of authorities in the country. If a country has a police force (and most countries do have a functioning police force, no matter how repressive their regime is), this is usually taken as evidence that protection is available, even though the evidence cited by the officials themselves proves the opposite and shows that the police force is either unable to provide the protection or is itself a threat to the person at risk. There are occasions when the juxtaposition of the objective evidence cited and the conclusion of the officials that is in blatant contradiction to that evidence is nothing short of breath taking. Again, the only plausible explanation is that officials are seeking to establish that there is no risk, instead of assessing the risk objectively. In other words, this is an adversarial relationship in which the purpose is to deny protection if any justification can be found. There are many examples of very elementary mistakes in the assessment of evidence which would be hilarious if the matter was not so serious. In one case a Vietnamese applicant was accused of incorrectly describing religious rituals and their significance. The applicant stated he was a Roman Catholic, the source used by the official who wrote the "reasons for refusal" was a Church of England publication. Apparently, the official who wrote the rejection document did not know that the Church of England is not part of the Roman Catholic Church and thereby was seemingly ignorant about the constitutional foundation of the United Kingdom.

Another tactic by the officials is to construct contradictions out of the statements by the applicant. It has to be remembered that most applicants have a low level of education and are not used to speaking in logically correct sentences. Once a contradiction (or "internal inconsistency" has been established, then this is used to attack other statements by the applicant even though there is no reason to assume that they are incorrect. For example, in the case of an applicant who claimed that he was North Korean his nationality was questioned because he was deemed to have given inconsistent information about unrelated matters. The fact that he only spoke Korean language seemed irrelevant, moreover the Home Office did not try to claim that he was Chinese, South Korean or that he had any other nationality and suggested he should be "returned" to South Korea which would only be possible if he was in fact North Korean. The purpose of the official who made these statements was apparently not to ascertain facts, but to besmirch the character of the applicant. Officials have also stated they would return North Korean applicants to North Korea, even though they know that this is neither legally nor physically possible. The purpose can only be to intimidate the applicants who have gone through very traumatic experiences and compel them to seek aid from the South Korean embassy to gain protection from the Republic of Korea.

There are various elements of the claims by applicants which are often disputed. Nationality is one of them. There are guidelines set down although various elements of the official guidance are kept confidential. If there is doubt about a person's nationality, the available information indicates that the officials will claim that the applicant has the nationality of a country to which they believe the applicant could easily be "returned" (even though he/she may not actually be a national of this country). For example, the Home Office has tried to return Syrians and Iranians to Iraq (including the Kurdish Region of Iraq), even though the applicants claimed (and the judge in the tribunal subsequently agreed) that they were not nationals of Iraq. Clearly applicants could not be returned to Syria and return to Iran is considered far more difficult and probably would be unsuccessful.

Similar observations apply to the disputes about the validity of a marriage. For example, Islamic marriages that have not resulted in the formal registration of a marriage are not legally valid in the United Kingdom. From the point of view of the authorities, if a marriage is to provide a basis to give person leave to enter the country and remain, it is not valid. On the other hand, if it provides the basis to return a couple to its country of origin, then all of a sudden it is considered valid, even though it is neither valid in the United Kingdom nor in the country of origin (eg. Pakistan). If an unmarried couple involves two persons from two different countries, then the authorities are not above demanding that the persons should marry so that they could meet the requirements of the immigration laws of one of the countries, even though the Home Office itself does its utmost to prevent or not recognize marriages for the purposes of immigration into the United Kingdom.

For younger persons, the age of the applicant is commonly disputed. Age is important when a person claims to be a minor. The level of support and the rules of dealing with this applicant are different if he/she is a minor, so it is common for age to be disputed, even though it is well known that there is no scientifically accurate way to determine a person's age to within greater accuracy than two years.

Claims to religious belief are also commonly disputed. Where the authorities derive their authority to assess whether someone is a

Christian, a Muslim or a faithful follower of Hoa Hao Buddhism, especially over and against leaders of these religious communities who write testimonials for the applicants is unclear. The assessment by the UK authorities generally ignores that the knowledge of facts and teaching as essential to religious faith is a Western cultural predisposition which is not shared by other cultures. Many persons from non-Western cultural backgrounds do not pay much attention to the facts or doctrines of religion but perceive religion as a cultural and communal activity. For example, most North Korean refugees in China join the Korean churches in China and become Christians, but their knowledge of even basic facts about Christianity is often poor. The religious knowledge displayed by officials in their assessments is itself usually poor and relies on peculiar external sources (in the sense that they are not authoritative sources recognized by members of religious communities), all indicators that the officials themselves have no direct personal knowledge of the faith communities concerned.

One issue that has received considerable press coverage is the issue of trafficking. Many asylum seekers are victims of trafficking, but the UK authorities insist on returning them to their home country despite the risks of re-trafficking. In the case of one Vietnamese female victim who had been trafficked for sexual exploitation the UK authorities acknowledged that she had been raped more than once, but they argued that she could return to Vietnam not despite, but because of this gruesome experience, on the basis that now she would know how avoid being re-trafficked, a factually false and morally completely unacceptable reasoning. There is no doubt that efforts to inhibit trafficking of persons to the United Kingdom is seriously hampered by the fact that the victims risk deportation if they report their traffickers. The situation is worse in relation to trafficking for labour which frequently forces the victims to engage in illegal activities such as cultivating cannabis plants. It is a common occurrence that these places are raided by the police, and the victims of trafficking are at risk of persecution. After they serve the prison sentence which has been imposed even in cases where judges acknowledged that the defendants had been coerced into the criminal activities, the UK authorities seek to deport them for having committed a crime punishable with a custodial sentence.

The asylum system is broken because the authorities that manage it show no evidence of a desire to support and protect refugees. It has become a branch of the UK immigration system whose main purpose is to minimize immigration and keep poor and needy persons out of the country. There is no penalty for rejecting applicants on spurious or false grounds or submitting false information to a tribunal as long as the decision is to reject. If asylum applicants are returned to their home country and subsequently experience persecution or are killed, no one involved in the decision process to return them suffers any consequences. Grounds are used for rejecting claimants even if they have been dismissed by tribunals on multiple occasions. Only the so-called country guidance cases can on occasion compel a modification in the arguments used.

This is not to say that every asylum claim should be automatically accepted. It is true that asylum seekers also lie, present forged documents and seek to obfuscate at various times. It can be argued that the country must have robust system that gives protection only to those who need it. But the purpose of the system as it operates now, judged by the way it is managed, is principally to prevent the country from being in violation of international law without honouring the spirit of the law. This assessment is an analysis of their actual conduct in specific cases using a review of published tribunal judgements where the views of the authorities (referred to as the respondent) is described in some detail. We expect that our governmental institutions behave fairly and honourably. In addition to a complete lack of accountability that is only somewhat constrained by the tribunals, there is very little hard information on what happens to failed asylum seekers after they are returned. But there is anecdotal evidence that returned asylum seekers have experienced severe persecution and some have been killed. There is no evidence that this information has any impact on official decision-making. The obvious way to reform this system would be to take the decisions on asylum applications out of the hands of immigration authorities and create completely separate institutions whose purpose is to positively seek to grant protection to those who genuinely need it.

Country evidence is critical in the assessment of any asylum claim. The purpose of this study is to review some of the common issues which frequently are the focus of asylum appeal cases in relation to applicants from South Asia and the Middle East. The focus is on Pakistan, Iraq and Iran and it covers a range of issues that give rise to asylum claims, such as the general security situation, the risk from terrorism and other forms of political violence, the risk to political opponents of governments, the risks in blood feuds and from the perceived violation of family honour, religious persecution and the risks faced by ethnic minorities. It is designed to be a resource to volunteers and professionals involved in supporting asylum seekers. If it helps even one asylum applicant to be given the protection that he/she needs and deserves, it will have served its purpose.

PART I
Pakistan

CHAPTER 2

Political Violence in Pakistan

Asylum claims submitted by Pakistan nationals usually fall into several different categories. The first are the risks due to political violence in Pakistan. The second relate to risks due the violation of family honour. These family conflicts can involve resistance against an arranged or forced marriage, divorce or relations with an unapproved partner. A third category has to do with religious persecution and the blasphemy law. This chapter discusses the various issues arising from political violence in Pakistan.

2.1 The risks of terrorist violence in Pakistan

Pakistan is passing through an extremely dangerous period of instability. The war in Afghanistan, the activities of Al Qaeda and ISIS and the efforts by the Taliban not only to regain control in Afghanistan, but to bring down the Pakistani state and replace it with a sharia based kalifate have led Pakistan to the point where in the words of Varun Vina and Anthony Cordesman, "the patterns of violence and stability indicate that Pakistan is approaching a perfect storm of threats, including rising extremism, a failing economy, chronic underdevelopment, and an intensifying war, resulting in unprecedented political, economic and social turmoil."[3]

The civilian government in government is to a significant extent dysfunctional. Repeated military rule has damaged the civilian institutions and the civilian governments have never been fully in control. But the military has only been able to play such a large role in the running of country due to the disenchantment of the population with its civilian rulers. Pakistani politicians do not put the country's interests before that of family or party. The focus on maximising personal gain, they continue to entrench feudal interests and corruptions is deeply embedded in the system of government.

Pakistani society in its entirety is terrorised by militant extremists. Their violence is wholly indiscriminate, and they attack police, soldiers as well as all civilians including women and children. They carry out bombing and suicide attacks on government agencies, in all manner of public places and even mosques. For example, on 1 April 2011 more than forty people were killed in a double suicide attack by the Taliban on the Sufi shrine in the Dera Ghazi Khan district in Punjab.[4] Also in 2011 Taliban insurgents attacked the Karachi naval base, resulting in the deaths of 12 people and the destruction of aircraft, allegedly in revenge for the death of Osama Bin Laden.[5] Another attack in revenge for the killing of bin Laden occurred on 25 June 2011 inside a police station in the Dera Ismail Khan District of Khyber Pakhtunkhwa.[6] In February 2015 a Taliban suicide bomber attacked a police station in Lahore, killing six.[7] In February 2017 a Taliban attack targeting the police in Lahore killed eleven persons.[8] In 2018 well over 100 major terrorist incidents have been reported, including the killing of eight Shia Muslims (including 2 women and a children) by a roadside bomb in Kurram Agency in the FATA on 30 January 2018, the killing of four Christian men in Quetta on 2 April 2018, and in 3 February 2018 eleven Pakistani Army soldiers were killed and 13 wounded in a suicide bombing near a Pakistani Army camp in Kabal area in Swat District of Khyber Pakhtunkhwa.[9] After the events of 9-11, the United States first demanded that the Taliban government in Afghanistan hand over Osama Bin Laden. When they refused, *Operation Enduring Freedom* was launched, and the Taliban were overthrown and Al Qaeda training camps were destroyed as Osama Bin Laden was forced to flee. The Pakistani government under President Musharraf decided to support the US in its campaign against the Taliban and Al Qaeda. As a result, the Pakistani state itself became the enemy of the Taliban and foreign Islamist fighters, who attempted to assassinate President

Musharraf himself, killed former Prime Minister Benazir Bhutto in Rawalpindi and conducted a range of attacks against Pakistani officials and security forces. The drone attacks by the United States with the cooperation and support of the Pakistani governments that involve agents on the ground to provide intelligence and target guidance have due to their success created a high degree of paranoia among the Taliban in Pakistan and efforts to root out spies, suspect agents for the US or the Pakistani government and provoked many *fatwahs* against alleged collaborators.

There are a many different extremist jihadist movements in Pakistan, and the Taliban themselves consist of several distinct organisations. The Tehrik-i-Taliban (TTP) are distinct from the Afghan Taliban, but they share a common ideology and common objectives. According to General Petraeus, the former commander of the US forces in Afghanistan, there is a symbiotic relationship between all these different al-Qaeda, the Pakistani Taliban, the Afghan Taliban, TNSM [Tehreek-e-Nafaz-e-Shariat-e-Mohammadi.[10] The Tehrik-i-Taliban have focused their activities on attacking and destroying the Pakistani state itself. They have carried out many suicide operations, such as for example the attack on the police training academy in Lahore in 2009,[11] the attack on the UN's World Food Programme Islamabad office on 5 October 2009,[12] the October 2009 attack on army headquarters in Rawalpindi[13] and the bombing of two Pakistani Navy buses in Karachi on 26 April 2011. They also target individuals, as evidenced by the execution of a former ISI Officer Colonel Imam that was captured on a video released by the TTP. There is further very considerable anecdotal evidence of the Taliban targeting fairly low-level individuals with death threats because they worked for the government or they were suspected of giving information to the ISI or the Americans.[14]

Although the Taliban and other Islamist extremists are most deeply entrenched in the FATA (Federally Administered Tribal Areas) and Khyber Pakhtunkhwa, they have people and sympathizers throughout Pakistan and have launched terrorist operations in the heartland of the Pakistani state (Rawalpindi, Islamabad, Karachi). For example, on 27 May 2009, the offices of the capital city police officer (CCPO) and the Inter-Services Intelligence (ISI) in Lahore were attacked with a 100 kg explosive device in a car. The attack killed at least 27 persons and injured 400 others. In 2008 it was reported that TTP kidnapped 70 people throughout Pakistan, including Karachi and Lahore, in order to raise funds.[15] In 2009 there was an attack on the Manawan police academy in Punjab province, killing 13 people and wounding over 100. Then TTP leader claimed responsibility for the attack in retaliation for US drone strikes in collaboration with the Pakistan government.[16] The reach that the TTP has throughout Pakistan was confirmed by the October 2009 attack on the army's headquarters at Rawalpindi. The attack was claimed to have been carried out by the "Punjabi faction" although the Pakistani army insisted the attack originated in South Waziristan.[17] The campaigns against the Taliban in the Swat Valley and the FATA by the Pakistani army have resulted in large numbers of internally displaced persons (IDP). There have been reports that the Taliban have shaved off their beards and have infiltrated the IDP camps as well as dispersed into other areas in Pakistan.[18] In particular, Taliban have entered Karachi (without joining the camps). There is also a Tehrik-i-Taliban Punjab (also called Punjabi Taliban). Especially in Southern Punjab there is a substantial militant presence and several thousand southern Punjabi are fighting in Waziristan and Afghanistan.[19] Although the threat of attacks from the Taliban is greater in the FATA, there is no part of Pakistan that is completely safe.[20]

The violent activities of the militant organisations that aim to bring about a collapse of the Pakistani state and its recreation as an Islamic caliphate have transformed Pakistan in what many consider the most dangerous country on earth. The conditions are ideal for terrorist networks to thrive because of political instability, the rivalry between political leaders and the armed forces, a highly developed network of radical Islamists, and abundance of anti-Western recruits, corrupt security services of limited competence. The violence including kidnappings, suicide attacks and bombings present a constant risk to the life of ordinary people. In view of the pervasive violence and political instability, Foreign Policy magazine in 2011 ranked Pakistan as number 12 in the "most failed states" in the world. The ambivalent attitude of the authorities to militant groups (partly combating them but also cultivating them as a tool of foreign policy towards Indian and

Afghanistan) has made Pakistan a "cockpit of terrorist violence".[21] In 2017 a new wave of violence started, as reported by The Independent: "More than 130 people have been killed in a wave of terror attacks that started on 13 February, when the Taliban's Jamaa-ul-Ahrar faction announced the start of a new campaign of violence against the government, security forces, the judiciary and secular political parties."[22] The problem is exacerbated by the activities of ISIS (Daesh) in Pakistan, increasing the risk of violence.

The Taliban are also known for kidnapping persons in order to extort money. British Asian in particular have been a target for kidnappers and the number of such incidents has been rising. If the attempt to extort money proves unsuccessful this may result in the death of the victim. For any foreigner or someone deemed to have a foreign association travelling to Pakistan involves serious risks.[23]

Violence by the Taliban against political figures and members of political parties has been a normal feature of the Pakistani political landscape for a number of years. There was an intense campaign in the run-up to the 2013 elections. A total of 148 terrorist attacks were reported across Pakistan between January 1 and May 15, The targets were political leaders and workers, election candidates, offices, public meetings and election rallies, as well as polling stations. It was reported that 170 people were killed and 743 injured. The Tehreek-e-Taliban Pakistan (TTP) and associated local Taliban and other militant groups were responsible for 108 attacks in which 156 people died and 665 injured 40 attacks were carried out by Baloch nationalist insurgents killing 14 people.[24] Extremist violence has continued in Pakistan. For example it was reported: "In 2016 an attack on Bacha Khan University in January 2016, which killed 21 people, highlighted the resiliency of the umbrella group'sability to carry out attacks. ..In April 2016, TTP splinter group Jamaat-ul-Ahrar … carried out a suicide bombing in a park in Lahore that targeted families celebrating Easter, killing at least seventy people and wounding over three hundred.[25]" In 2018 well over 100 major terrorist incidents have been reported, including the killing of eight Shia Muslims (including 2 women and a children) by a roadside bomb in Kurram Agency in the FATA on 30 January, the killing of four Christian men in Quetta on 2 April 2018, and in 3 February 2018 eleven Pakistani Army soldiers were killed and 13 wounded in a suicide bombing near a Pakistani Army camp in Kabal area in Swat District of Khyber Pakhtunkhwa.[26]

2.2 Politics and violence in Pakistan

This section provides some country background information that shows how local members of political parties are frequently involved in political violence.

Pakistan is passing through an extremely dangerous period of instability. The war in Afghanistan, the activities of Al Qaeda and the efforts by the Taliban not only to regain control in Afghanistan, but to bring down the Pakistani state and replace it with a sharia based kalifate have led Pakistan to the point where in the words of Varun Vina and Anthony Cordesman, "the patterns of violence and stability indicate that Pakistan is approaching a perfect storm of threats, including rising extremism, a failing economy, chronic underdevelopment, and an intensifying war, resulting in unprecedented political, economic and social turmoil."[27]

The civilian government in government is to a significant extent dysfunctional. Repeated military rule has damaged the civilian institutions and the civilian governments have never been fully in control. But the military has only been able to play such a large role in the running of country due to the disenchantment of the population with its civilian rulers. Pakistani politicians do not put the country's interests before that of family or party. The focus on maximising personal gain, they continue to entrench feudal interests and corruptions is deeply embedded in the system of government.

Pakistan's political system is based on patronage and kinship, not ideology. As Anatol Lieven has observed:

"With the exception of the MQM and the religious parties, all of Pakistan's 'democratic' political parties are congeries of landlords, clan chieftains and urban bosses seeking state patronage for themselves and their followers and vowing allegiance to particular national individuals and dynasties."[28] In this sense, main stream political parties, are better described as political groupings formed by a chain of political fiefdoms based on patronage in which power is concentrated on particular families who seek to maintain their power within their network. The PPP is founded around the Bhutto dynasty, the PML-N around the Sharif dynasty, while the Awami National Party is based on the Wali Khan dynasty. The PML-Q was formed as a breakaway group from the PML-N under the aegis of former President Musharraf and is led by the Chaudhury brothers from Gujrat.

Party politics in Pakistan is defined by intense personal loyalties to a particular leading family and to local power brokers. Anatol Lieven recounts a conversation on this issue:

"Of course, So-and-So Khan would like to join the ruling party; but he can't because the Sharifs [or the Bhuttos] will never forgive him for what he did to them when he was in government".[29]

It is not surprising that in a country like Pakistan, where local and national politics is dominated by intense power struggles and personal rivalries, political violence is common. Political parties are constantly engaged in efforts to personally destroy their opponents, either by forcing them to face legal proceedings that would put them in prison, or any other means that are available, including violent attacks. Although legal prohibitions against the use of violence against individuals are in place, there remains an acceptance with in sections of the population of the legitimacy of the use of violence against family members who are deemed to have defiled family honour (honour killings), religious violence (jihad) and other forms of political violence. This in the first quarter of 2012, 517 incidents of political violence were reported in Pakistan, affecting all regions. In these incidents, a total of 957 persons lost their lives, 927 were injured and 141 kidnapped. If such events were to occur in a Western country, they would be considered to constitute a political crisis of catastrophic proportions, but in Pakistan this is in line with the experience since the creation of the state.[30]

The so-called mainstream parties are not cohesive organisations, but instead they are a chain of local fiefdoms in which many individuals seek to establish their own power and networks of patronage and where it is common for groups to split off from the main parties to form their own political organisations.

There have been numerous incidents involving every party of the political spectrum, including the PPP (Pakistan Peoples Party).

In Karachi in particular, the PPP has been involved a bitter power struggle with the MQM (Muttahida Qaumi Movement) and the ANP (Awami National Party) that has involved attacks by violent gangs loyal to the PPP and gruesome acts of violence perpetrated by various parties, including the Taliban and other extremists. Although Karachi is probably the most violent city in Pakistan, these kinds of power struggles and acts of violence occur throughout Pakistan, including Punjab.[31]

The enmity between the PML-N (Pakistan Muslim League) and PML-Q is well documented. The PLM-Q (Quaid-e-Azam) was founded by dissidents from the Pakistan Muslim League that supported the 1999 coup by General Musharraf against the then and recent Prime Minister of Pakistan, Nawaz Sharif. Given their history, Sharif and Musharraf have been bitter enemies since the coup which followed an attempt by Sharif to dismiss Musharraf. Physical violence between members of the PLM-Q and PML-N has been documented repeatedly in newspaper reports and even videos on YouTube. In the election in 2013, PMLQ MPA Candidate Rubina Sulehri was recorded calling for violence in her speech. Violence involving these political rivals was widely reported during the 2013 elections and since. For example: "It was revealed in an official report received by 'The News' and presented to the president and prime minister that a heinous series of killings was witnessed during the 20- day electoral campaign. The report said that 81 persons were killed and 437 injured in 119 violent incidents in the 20- day electoral campaign. [...] The Awami National Party (ANP), MQM, JI [Jamaat-e-Islami], JUI [Jamiat Ulema-e-Islam], QWP [Qaumi Watan Party], PML-N, PML-Q, PML-F, Jafferia Alliance, BNP [Balochistan National Party], Sunni Tehrik and PTI along with 16 other parties were made target of election violence. [...] It was revealed in the report that the ANP and MQM were the most-affected parties with regard to terrorism attacks."[32] In Punjab a man putting up an election poster for the PLM-Q was shot dead.[33] In 2008 there was a Taliban suicide attack against the leader of the Awami National Party and he left the country temporarily.[34]

The threats again the Awami National Party have continued since they reached such a level in 2013 that the Awami National Party asked for support to safeguard its security against the Taliban, without any result. The press reported that there multiple attacks against party workers, with the ANP suffering by far the most casualties.[35] Thus the press reported an attack against a leading ANP politician: "A bomb exploded close to the home of a prominent provincial minister in restive northwest Pakistan on Tuesday, wounding six people including three children, police said... Mr. Hussain, a member of the province's ruling Awami National Party (ANP) whose son was killed by Taliban militants, was 25 kilometres (15 miles) away in Peshawar at the time of the blast, police said... Mr. Hussain is well known in Pakistan for speaking out against militants. In July 2010 the Taliban shot dead his only son Mian Rashid Hussain, 28, as he travelled home. The Tehreek-e-Taliban Pakistan have vowed to kill politicians from the secular ANP and in December a suicide bomber killed Hussain's colleague Bashir Bilour, the number two minister in Khyber Pakhtunkhwa, along with eight other people at a political meeting.[36]

Since 2009 over 1000 workers and leaders of the Awami National Party have been killed by the Taliban.[37] According to the 2017 report of the Asian Foundation, those associated with the Awami National Party are targeted throughout Pakistan.[38] Membership and work for the ANP puts a person at serious risk of violent attack by extremists.

One case of political violence that received a great deal of attention was that Muhammad Farooq Khan, a Pakistani academic. He was a psychiatrist and at the time of his untimely death vice-chancellor of the University of Swat. He was a known "moderate" and condemned suicide attacks as un-Islamic. According to a press report: "Police quoted eyewitnesses as saying that two armed men entered Dr Khan's clinic, in Baghdad locality, saying that they were patients. But as soon as they saw the doctor, they opened fire, killing him on the spot. Dr Farooq's assistant, Mohammad Saleem, was shot dead by the assailants when he offered resistance. The assailants escaped."[39]

According to a prominent Pakistani newspaper: "Dr Farooq presented an enlightened version of Islamic teachings, which turned many against him. He was a great source of inspiration for students. He supported many students financially. He received many threats trying to warn him, but his commitment was never weakened. He was a valuable asset to Pakistan, a man of reason who spoke his mind without fear. He strived hard through his books and lectures to eliminate misconceptions about Islam from the minds of Muslims and non-Muslims."[40]

A particular example of violence involving political parties in Pakistan is the MQM. The current MQM-A (Muttahida Qaumi Movement) is a secular political party that emerged from the Muhajir Qaumi Movement founded by Altaf Hussein in 1984 as a student movement (originally called the Muhajir Student organisation) to defend the rights of Mohajirs. The Mohajir were migrants from India who were Muslim and spoke Urdu, they and their descendants make up 60 percent of Karachi's population of twelve million. In 1997 the name of the party changed its name. It removed the term Mohajir and replaced with the term Muttahida (united). The MQM-A has traditionally been the dominant political force in the city of Karachi, it is the second largest party in Sindh and was the fourth-largest party in the National Assembly of Pakistan. The party has been a key coalition partner with the ruling Party in Pakistan's federal government throughout most of the election terms since the late 1980s. The first of these coalitions was with the MQM the coalition government headed by Benazir Bhutto's Pakistan People's Party (PPP), which came to power in elections after the death of military leader General Zia ul-Haq. The MQM's rise to national prominence and influence at the level of federal politics was accompanied by increasing violence between the MQM and Sindhi groups that routinely broke out in major Sindh cities, especially Karachi.[41]

Towards the end of 1991 serious disagreements between Altaf Hussain and the then MQM's two prominent militant leaders, Afaq Ahmed and Aamir Khan came to the fore and resulted in a formal split in June 1992 after Pakistani security forces launched *Operation Cleanup* in Karachi. Ahmed and Khan launched the MQM Haqiqi (MQM-H), which literally means the "real MQM". The dissidents attached Haqiqi meaning real or authentic in Urdu as a suffix to the MQM acronym as an assertion of the outfit's legitimacy. This split was followed by the creation of further splinter groups and the outbreak of severe violence. Internecine clashes within the Mohajir community were accompanied by targeted killings in which terrorists of one faction attacked members of the other. Fighting between the factions of the MQM and Sindhi nationalists resulted in almost daily killings in Karachi and the violence extended to other cities. By July 1995 the rate of murders had increased to 10 per day. In June 1997 the headquarters of the MQM-H was attacked by terrorists from the MQM-A sparking off yet another series of attacks as the factions target each other.[42]

The violence in Karachi and other cities peaked in 1997 and began to abate somewhat as soldiers and police intensified their crackdowns on the MQM-A and the rival groups (Jane's 14 Feb 2003). Pakistani forces staged so-called "encounter killings" in which they shot MQM activists and then blamed it on militants. It was after a crackdown in 1997 that the MQM-A adopted its current name as the United National Movement.[43] In 1992 MQM-A leader Hussein fled to the United Kingdom, where he was granted asylum in 1999. He left Pakistan after an arrest warrant for murder was issued against him. [44]

Although the tactics of the Pakistani security forces and the general level of rivalry and violence between various radical groups made it difficult to always correctly attribute the violence, nevertheless the MQM-A was routinely involved in various crimes of violence. After a crackdown by the army in 1992, facilities for the torture and killing of dissident members and political activists from other groups were discovered. According to Amnesty International, there were also reports from the Pakistan People's Party and other political groups that some of the members had been tortured and murdered by the MQM-A.[45]

The MQM-A also has a history of intimidating journalists (as do other groups accused of using violence against their opponents). For example in 1990 MQM leader Hussein issued threats against the editor of the monthly magazine Newsline after it published an article alleging the use of torture by the MQM-A against dissidents.[46] An article by journalist Zafar Abbas published in 1991 described the development of the various factions in the movement was followed by an attack against him in Karachi during which he was seriously assaulted. MQM activists also attacked vendors selling Dawn, an English language newspaper in Pakistan, and other publications they disapproved of.[47] The practice of attacking journalist who report unfavourably about the MQM-A has continued to the present day, according to Amnesty International. For example, in 2010 Wali Khan

Barbar, a reporter for the TV station Geo, was killed by the MQM-A. It is reported that news outfits and TV stations are infiltrated by radical groups, including the MQM-A for the purpose of influencing the news and enable to target the hostile journalists.[48]

A report by The Economist has characterised the behaviour by the MQM in Karachi as follows: "The MQM has run a huge and violent criminal racket in the city alongside its political wing... heavies ... would demand payments of up to $10,000 from shopkeepers every few months... operating street by street, the MQM had become a master of the extortion game."[49] Since 2013, the Pakistani authorities have used the rangers to crack down on criminal activists in the MQM and the Pakistan People's Party (PPP), using fairly brutal tactics in the process. In August 2015 the MQM-A announced the resignation of all of its MPs in the federal National Assembly. The MQM-A is leaving politics but seeks to re-enter parliament on the basis of a deal that includes the end of their persecution by the authorities. This is not the first time they have engaged in this kind of political manoeuvre.

The MQM-A and the MQM-H have been bitter rivals to the present day. The MQM-A believes the Haqiqi faction was supported by the Pakistani government in order to weaken the original movement. As the MQM-A has faced crackdowns supported by the Rangers, it accuses the Haqiqi faction of collaborating with them. The leader of the MQM-A claims that the MQM-H does not have any political agenda of its own and is involved in extortion rackets. The MQM-H on the other hand clams that the MQM-A has betrayed its original constituency, the Mohajirs and is not helping to address the continuing socio-economic and political injustices they suffer. It has claimed that if these issues are not dealt with demand for a separate province within Pakistan would intensify to protect the Mohajirs.

According to a report by the South Asia Terrorism Portal published by the Institute for Conflict Management "the MQM (H) has survived without the sort of political mandate enjoyed by the Altaf Hussain group and controls certain neighbourhoods in Karachi by force. In 1997-98, the MQM (A), which as a coalition partner of then Prime Minister Nawaz Sharif's, Pakistan Muslim League, had repeatedly accused the MQM (H) of creating 'no-go areas' in Karachi, localities where MQM (H) activists were preventing MQM

(A) activists from entering. But MQM (H) leader Afaq Ahmed while denying the existence of "no-go areas" maintains that it is a "baseless term". According to the Haqiqi faction, these are the areas where the MQM-A and his cadres have unleashed a reign of terror. News reports also mention that Malir, Landhi, Shah Faisal Colony and Korangi areas which were the strong holds of MQM (A) till a short while ago are now under the control of the Haqiqi faction."[50]

The Haqqiqi movement declined to some extent as it failed to achieve the degree of political support of its rival and its founder and leader Ahmed was arrested in 2004 and accused of several murders. After nearly eight years of imprisonment, he had been found guilty of any crime. On 17 December 2011, the Sindh High Court declared that Ahmed's imprisonment under the "Maintenance of Public Order" provisions was illegal. It ordered that he was to be freed.

The Muttahida Quami Movement (MQM) was an ally of former president Pervez Musharraf who came to power by a military coup. However, the MQM is considered an enemy of the Bhutto family's Pakistani People Party (PPP), which was in power until the recent elections. This made the MQM a target for state sponsored violence. Staniland cited the example of Altaf Hussain, the leader of the MQM, who fears for his safety. He has been living in exile in London since the 1990s and participates in the political process by making speeches through telephone and webcam during MQM rallies in Pakistan. While political opponents and their families may be targeted, all those who engage in the political process including activists, academics and journalists and their families can become targets of militias or state - sponsored violence in the continuing struggle for political influence and power in Pakistan.

The 2013 elections in Pakistan were again marred by violence between the party organisations. According to a report in Pakistan Today, in relation to the city of Karachi, "DG Rangers Major General Rizwan Akhtar said that militant wings of political parties are responsible for the ongoing violence in the city."[51] There is also clear evidence that the PML-N was a particular target of violence.[52]

5.4.12 The 2013 elections in Pakistan took place amid a veritable orgy of killings - minority groups, civilians and military personnel were all target by various extremists, according to the respected expert

Ahmed Rashid. As the number of targeted assassinations of leading politicians increased, it became ever clearer that the government and the security forces were unable to contain the violence. It was estimated that during this time period an average of 10 to 20 people a day were being killed in the major cities such as Karachi, Quetta, Lahore and Peshawar.[53] The preparedness of members of political parties to use violence against each other was demonstrated by the fact that between January 1 and May 15, 2013, 128 leaders and workers of different political parties were killed and 142 injured in 97 reported incidents. These referred to political violence not from terrorists but occurred between supporters and workers of different political parties during the same period of time. The situation was worst in Sindh province where such violence by members of political parties and their militant sections resulted in 97 deaths, largely of party workers and leaders of different political parties (70 in Karachi alone). In Balochistan 16 people were killed and another 15 injured in inter-party political violence.[54]

The government of Nawaz Sharif conducted a clean-up operation in Karachi that targeted many MQM officials. In 2018 the MQM-A boycotted the elections. Another faction called the MQM-P was formed which under the leadership of Farooq Sattar who had previously been kidnapped by the Pakistan rangers as part of the "clean-up" instigated against the MQM which took part and fielded candidates in the elections 2018.

The MQM still has significant influence in some parts of Pakistan, especially in Karachi. Members of this party would have sufficient influence to have the cooperation of the local security services to locate individuals throughout Pakistan, though as was pointed out above, this is a low threshold and even bribery would suffice to achieve this objective. More importantly, members of the MQM have been known for becoming involved in very serious violence to such an extent that they are deemed to be a threat to the state.

2.3 Treatment of dissenters on Pakistan's Kashmir policy

A very separate political issue in which individuals have been at risk of violence from the authorities as well as jihadists is the issue of Kashmir which is fundamental to Pakistan's national security. It is the central driver of Pakistan's conflict with India that has persisted ever since the creation of Pakistan. This persistent conflict in South Asia has given rise to a large military establishment in Pakistan which has become a state within a state. But the persistence of the dominant and unaccountable position of the military establishment in Pakistan is contingent on and justified by this persistent conflict with a militarily superior neighbour. Without it the dominant role and status of the military establishment in Pakistani politics would not be tolerated. Leaving aside radical Islam, there is no greater political threat to the ruling elite in Pakistan than questioning the dominant narrative on Kashmir.[55]

The region which in the United Nations is referred to as "Pakistani-controlled Kashmir" are two entities called Gilgit-Baltistan and Azad Jammu and Kashmir. The Indian state of Jammu and Kashmir is adjacent to Azad Jammu and Kashmir (the two territories are separated by the so-called "line of control") and is referred to in Pakistan as "Indian-occupied Kashmir".[56]

There have been three wars over Kashmir between India and Pakistan, as well as more low-level operations that have continued over a period of time. In 1947 the region of Azad Jammu and Kashmir was occupied by the Pakistani army and irregular fighters (militants) after the former Princely State had been formally linked with India. As Pakistan has pushed for Kashmir (a predominantly Muslim region) to be wholly integrated into Pakistan, the two countries went to war in 1965 and 1999 and have been involved in various skirmishes, for example over control of the Siachen Glacier. In 1999 the Kargil incident nearly provoked a full-scale war as militants and Pakistani paramilitary units moved across the line of control. Pakistan controls about 37% of the whole of the region described as Kashmir. Control over all of Kashmir is the most important objective of Pakistani national security policy since 1947.[57]

Militants and terrorists have been supported by the Pakistani government as proxy fighters in the war over Kashmir on numerous occasions and these activities by the Inter-Service Intelligence (ISI) and army has spawned various jihadist movements that have since extended their activities beyond the Kashmir region. Even though the Pakistani government now disavows these militants, there has been a strong connection between them and the ISI which continues to the present day.[58]

In August 2019 a serious crisis broke out in relation to the Kashmir issue. Indian-administered Kashmir had a special status within India since the foundation of India and Pakistan and the division of the Kashmir. This status had been codified by Article 370 of the constitution of India which gave Indian-administered Kashmir a substantial degree of autonomy and independence with respect to all matters except foreign affairs and defence. According to a BBC Report: "On 5 August, India revoked that seven-decade-long privileged status - as the governing party, the Bharatiya Janata Party (BJP), had promised in its 2019 election manifesto. The Hindu nationalist BJP has long opposed Article 370 and had repeatedly called for its abolishment. Telephone networks and the internet were cut off in the region in the days before the presidential order was announced. Public gatherings were banned, and tens of thousands of troops were sent in. Tourists were told to leave Kashmir under warnings of a terror threat."[59]

The decision by the Indian government and parliament provoked very sharp and hostile reactions in Pakistan. As Al Jazeera reported: "A joint sitting of parliament was scheduled for Tuesday morning in the capital Islamabad. Pakistan's Prime Minister Imran Khan was due to address the session, a statement from his office said. The Pakistan army chief also met his top commanders in Rawalpindi on Tuesday, with the military spokesperson confirming in a statement that «Pakistan never recognised the sham Indian efforts to legalise its occupation of Jammu & Kashmir through article 370 or 35-A decades ago». «Pakistan Army firmly stands by the Kashmiris in their just struggle to the very end. We are prepared and shall go to any extent to fulfil our obligations in this regard,» said army chief General Qamar Javed Bajwa."[60]

Pakistan announced that it would halt trade with India and the top Indian diplomat in Islamabad was expelled while Pakistan's top representative in New Delhi was withdrawn in response to India's decision to unilaterally eliminate the autonomy of Kashmir. The Pakistani government, which also claims the restive region of Kashmir, said it would recall its own chief diplomat based in New Delhi. Thus, it was reported: A statement from a national security committee headed by the Pakistani prime minister, Imran Khan, said the changes would be put in place because of "illegal actions" by the Indian government regarding Kashmir, which has a Muslim majority. Mr. Khan denounced Prime Minister Narendra Modi of India, accusing his government of promoting "an ideology that puts Hindus above all other religions and seeks to establish a state that represses all other religious groups." The statement on Wednesday from the committee headed by Mr. Khan said that India's stripping of Kashmiri autonomy would also be raised by Pakistan with the United Nations Security Council, which recognizes the region as disputed. In addition to ending bilateral trade, which has been valued at several billion dollars annually, and downgrading diplomatic ties, Pakistani officials threatened to close the country's airspace to Indian aircraft. The statement said all bilateral agreements would also be reviewed."[61] All these actions by Pakistan have to be seen in the context that Pakistan views Indian-administered Kashmir as an occupied territory that properly belongs to Pakistan. The actions by India are correctly perceived as a move to integrate the Indian-administered territory of Kashmir properly into India and thereby prevent and future change of the territorial status quo. This action is seen as contrary to one of the most central key national objectives of Pakistan.

The context of these recent events is a crisis between India and Pakistan over Kashmir when at least 40 Indian security forces were killed by terrorist in Indian-administered Kashmir were killed in a major terrorist attack. India suspected that the terrorists were proxy forces of the Pakistani state, as has been the case in previous attacks on the other side of the so-called line-of-control (LOC) that separates India from Pakistan. As a consequence, there were military skirmishes between Indian and Pakistan forces that resulted in the downing of an Indian jet. The Prime Minister of Pakistan warned that there was a risk that the most recent crisis would escalate into a war between India and Pakistan.[62] In other words, the Kashmir situation is currently at the centre of an international crisis that threatens to escalate into a major military confrontation. It is too early to have clear evidence on the effect of this tense situation on the activities of the UKPNP. But given that the political activities of the UKPNP threaten on of the key interests of the Pakistani state (see next section), it is fair to assume that Pakistani authorities will not tolerate and will seek to suppress any kind of political activity that will question the official narrative on Kashmir under such extreme circumstances as prevail at present.

Dissent on the official stance on Kashmir has been exercised by the United Kashmir People's National Party which is a political party and advocacy group based in Pakistani occupied Kashmir.[63] Its main policy objective is to support total independence of a united Kashmir both from Pakistan and India. This means they not only call for Pakistan to relinquish part of its territory, but also to abandon the most central goal of its foreign policy since the foundation of the state. They explicitly challenge the official narrative in relation to Kashmir.[64] They accuse the government in Islamabad of violating democratic norms, colonialism and by implication serious crimes against humanity.[65] The party holds public meetings in support of their cause, and events have been held and disrupted by security services in the past.[66]

According to the reports of an international conference held in Brussels, Sardar Shaukat Ali Kashmiri is the chairman of the UKPNP. According to reports by the Hindustan Times, Kashmiri was exiled from Pakistan in 1999 and since May 2006 has settled in Switzerland. He conducts his activities as chair of the UKPNP from exile and seeks to give his organisation and its objective an international profile as secretary general of the International Kashmir Alliance.[67]

There is evidence that the Interservices Intelligence (ISI), Pakistan's Intelligence Service, has systematically persecuted the UKPNP. The UKPNP organised seminars in different cities of Azad Kashmir on human rights violations and right of self-determination of the people of Kashmir, Gilgit & Baltistan and demanded the exit of Pakistan Army from POK (Pakistan occupied Kashmir). The UKPNP organised many demonstrations against theo-fascism and

Pakistan's proxy war with India. UKPNP Chairman Sardar Shaukat Ali Kashmiri was abducted by ISI in 1994 and 1998. UKPNP and other like-minded parties and groups demonstrated against his illegal confinement and detention throughout Azad Kashmir and Pakistan. Eventually Kashmiri was forced to leave the country where it was no longer safe for him to remain.[68]

According to an investigation by M. Ilyas Khan from BBC News, the persecution of the UKPNP continues. The report states: "Ismat Karim gives a harrowing account of a recent 20-day detention in what he calls a 'torture cell'. Mr Karim says he was held along with two other residents of Pakistan-administered Kashmir and describes how they were 'punished and interrogated' in turn for half-an-hour every evening. 'They would whip us with lashes and ask the whereabouts of a person whose name we had never heard.' They were given no reason for their arrest." Karim was an activist in the UKPNP. "He says that he had been rounded up by Pakistan's powerful Inter-Services Intelligence (ISI)." Another case is that of Abdul Majeed who as a student involved in politics and advocating an independent Kashmir was "implicated in as many as 47 different criminal offences ranging from murder and treason to rioting and theft. 'For three months I was in a police lock-up. When the court set aside one case, they would bring another one against me', he says."[69]

There are many reports that in Pakistan and in particular in Kashmir the Intelligence Service (ISI) detains people arbitrarily, resulting in significant public protests against the detentions and eventually the release of at least some of the detainees.[70] The police also detains members of the anti-Kashmir activists from the UKPNP or the JKLF.

The police often become actively involved in the persecution of members of the party which is considered to be a threat to national security. Police involvement is based on preserving public order (eg. disrupting demonstrations or public events deemed to be against the interests of the state) and the police is answerable to the relevant ministry, whereas the ISI is answerable to the leadership of the armed forces.

There is no doubt that the political activities on behalf of the UKPNP or makes individuals a target for persecution by the

Pakistani government as represented by the police or the ISI. There is considerable evidence that the authorities have targeted members of the UKPNP as their activities are considered a threat to national security. Various members have been arrested and interrogated and persecuted by the ISI or the police.[71] Their methods of interrogation typically involve coercive methods which are commonly described as torture.[72]

The ISI is charged with foreign and domestic intelligence. Its domestic political activities range from managing to supressing political opposition. A significant aspect of its role is the surveillance of its cadre, foreigners, the media, foreign diplomats accredited to Pakistan, Pakistani diplomats serving outside the country, dissidents abroad and the interception and monitoring of communications. The ISI is known to monitor the activities of the UKPNP abroad.[73]

It is also common for religious judges to issue fatwās against members of the party. A fatwā is a nonbinding legal opinion on a point of Islamic law. It is given by a qualified jurist in response to a question posed by a private individual, judge or government. A jurist issuing fatwas is referred to as a mufti. It can be abused by extremists to justify acts of violence against its target as his political activities have been judged to be un-Islamic, although such a judgement does not have to be accepted by Muslims.

It is also common for first information reports (FIR) against UKPNP members to be lodged with the police. A First Information Report (FIR) is a written document prepared by the police based on information a cognizable offence and it can result in the initiation of prosecution and an arrest warrant. It is important to note that the information contained in FIRs are based on information provided by a member of the general public and their content is not verified or necessarily true, but they are evidence that someone has issued an accusation against another individual. The police often become actively involved in the persecution of members of the party which is considered to be a threat to national security. But police involvement is based on preserving public order (eg. disrupting demonstrations or public events deemed to be against the interests of the state) and the police is answerable to the relevant ministry, whereas the ISI is answerable to the leadership of the armed forces. An arrest warrant would be enforced by the police, but not by the ISI. It is almost universally the case the persons arrested for the political offences are tortured in custody by the police or the ISI.[74] If the police is involved in political persecution this may result in the issue of a First Information Report against the target for what is called a "cognizable offence" that permits the police to arrest a person without an arrest warrant. An arrest warrant would be issued by a court when a case has been submitted to the court. It is common for the police to issue "bogus FIRs" and ask for arrest warrants in cases of political persecution.[75] The "fake FIRs" contain accusations known not to be true or not to constitute properly "cognizable offences" (i.e. the penal code is inappropriately applied). False registration or non-registration of FIRs is very common (affecting 100,000s of cases in Punjab province alone) and has been identified as one of the main problems of the system.[76] Advocates for an independent Kashmir claim that there have been cases of "fake FIRs" against their supporters.[77]

It is a peculiar aspect of the Kashmir issue that this is one issue on which there has been agreement between the Taliban and other jihadists and the Pakistani government has been the issue of Kashmir. Indeed, the Pakistani government actively used and collaborated with jihadist extremists, using the Lashkar-e-Toiba as proxy fighters against India in their pursuit of sovereignty over Kashmir.

Lashkar-e-Toiba (also known as Jama'at-ud-Da'awa) was formed in 1990 in the Kunar province of Afghanistan. It is based in Muridke near Lahore in Pakistan and is headed by its founder and Amir, Professor Hafiz Muhammad Saeed. The organisation was officially banned by Gen. Pervez Musharraf in Pakistan on January 12, 2002, but unofficially collaboration between the LeT and the Pakistani intelligence services ISI continued.[78]

One of the LeT's primary objective has been to challenge India's sovereignty over the State of Jammu and Kashmir, and it was actively supported by the Pakistani government in this for some time. The Lashkar's 'agenda', as outlined in a pamphlet titled "Why are we waging jihad" includes the restoration of Islamic rule over all parts of India. It also promotes a union of all Muslim majority regions in countries that surround Pakistan. In addition, terrorist operations in the State of Jammu and Kashmir, it has been involved in Chechnya and other parts of Central Asia.[79] The LeT was responsible for the terror attack on Mumbai in 2008.[80]

LeT has clearly global ambitions, even if its capacities to realise them remain limited. According the Amir Hafiz Saeed, the purpose of Jihad is to carry out a sustained struggle for the dominance of Islam in the entire world and to eliminate the evil forces. The Lashkar-e-Toiba rejects democracy and nationalism. It considers it the duty of every one of its adherents to protect and defend the interests of Muslims all over the world where Muslims are under the rule of non-Muslim in the democratic system.[81]

LeT adheres to the Ahl-e-Hadith principles of Sunni Wahhabism. Therefore, one of its central objectives is to establish a universal Islamic caliphate and gradually recovering all lands that were once under Muslim rule. LeT was founded at the suggestion of Osama Bin Laden and has always been a strong ideological ally of al-Qaeda. The goal to recover "lost Muslim lands" in Asia and Europe has result in involvements by LeT in diverse places such as Afghanistan, the Palestinian territories, Spain, Chechnya, Kosovo, and Eritrea.[82]

Harkat-ul-Jihad-i-Islami (HUJI) is a transnational terrorist organisation based in Pakistan.[83] It has an extensive network and organisation structure that extends across Pakistan and into Indian-held Kashmir and Bangladesh. They are also active in Chechnya, Uzbekistan, and China (Xinjiang Province). The branch is in Bangladesh is considered to be relatively autonomous from the organisation based in Pakistan.[84] For a time HUJI received support from the Interservice Intelligence Services (ISI) in Pakistan but was banned in mid-2004. After that it also operated under the name Harkat-ul-Mujahideen al-Ami.[85]

It is the avowed goal of HUJI to impose the supremacy of Islam on the world. It also sees itself as "the second line of defence for all Muslim states" against outside non-Muslin aggressors.[86] The HUJI was involved in the fight of the Mujahedin against the Soviet invasion of Afghanistan and its founder was killed by Soviet forces in June 1985. While the Taliban were in power in Afghanistan, the central secretariat of HUJI was based in Kabul. Since then it has moved to Waziristan and Bonir. Although it is a distinct organisation, it is closely connected to the Afghan Taliban, Al Qaeda and the Pakistani

Taliban and some of its leaders simultaneously serve in key roles in these movements.

The organizational structure of HUJI has the following elements: Dawat-o-Irshad (preaching), military and training camps, finance and media and publications.[87] HUJI is active throughout at least 40 provinces in Pakistan. It is closely associated with the Taliban in Pakistan as well as Al Qaeda and has closely cooperated with the main jihadi groups in Pakistan.[88]

HUJI has been involved in major battles inside India and has recruited large numbers of mujahedeen to carry out the struggle in Indian-held Kashmir. Their fighters are recruited from many parts of Pakistan, Afghanistan, and Central Asia. The majority of fighters have been recruited from Pakistan Kashmir and Punjab.[89]

HUJI follows the Deobandi version of Islam. It is seeking to enable a renaissance of a new Islamic era and struggle to free Muslims from the confinement of the "east and west". It opposes un-Islamic style of politics and supports jihad far and wide until all occupied regions of the Muslims are freed. Islam is the only code of life. It establishes madrassas in order to educate young people in true paths of Islam.[90]

HUJI developed close relationships with the Afghan mujahedeen and in particular the Taliban. Many members of HUJI served in the Taliban army and government. Three Taliban ministers and 22 judges were from HUJI. After the fall of Taliban HUJI maintained relations with Mullah Omar, the Taliban leader, who is now believed to be in Pakistan.[91]

HUJI also has very close links with Al Qaeda both during the Taliban rule in Afghanistan and beyond. It was also funded and supported by the Pakistani secret services (the ISI).[92] Qari Saifullah Akktar, the amir (leader) of HUJI, was also "the operational head of Al Qaeda" in Pakistan.[93] Muhammad Ilyas Kashmiri was the operational commander of HuJI and head of Brigade 313, while at the same time considered to by US intelligence a major figure in Al Qaeda. He was killed by a U.S. drone strike in June 2011, his death was confirmed by Al Qaeda some time later.[94]

HUJI has been involved in terrorist operations throughout South Asia. Among its notable operations, HUJI was responsible for was the suicide bombing of the U.S. Consulate in Karachi, Pakistan on 2 March 2006, which killed four people, including U.S. diplomat David Foy, and injured 48 others. HUJI was also responsible for terrorist attacks in India including the May 2007 Hyderabad mosque attack, which killed 16 and injured 40, and the March 2006 Varanasi attack, which killed 25 and injured 100.[95] Off-shoots from HUJI have also been responsible for murderous campaigns against Sh'ia Muslims in Pakistan, underlining the extreme violence that members of this group are frequently engaged in.[96]

HUJ is one of the principal jihadist terrorist movements in South Asia, with a broad geographic reach, a presence throughout Pakistan and beyond, with a particular focus on Kashmir and operations in India. It is a very violent and ruthless organisation, it shares many of the personnel, ideas, goals and tactics with Al Qaeda and the Taliban and poses a serious threat to the security of Pakistan and neighbouring countries. Given their special efforts to fight the Indians over Kashmir, the HUJ would be a threat to the a member of the UKPNP.

The Hizb-ul-Mujahedeen ("party of holy warriors") was founded by Ahsan Dar in 1989 and is a Kashmiri separatist group involved in terrorist activities and designated by India and the European Union as a terrorist organisation. It is believed that the current leader of Hizb-ul- Mujahedeen, Sayeed Salahudeen, maintains constant contact with the ISI. Indeed, Salahudeen confirmed in an interview in 2012 that his organisation had been backed by the Pakistani government. Given their attitude to the Kashmir issue, their involvement in terrorist violence and their relation to the ISI, it is likely that they would seek to threaten political activists from the UKPNP.[97] The case of the above-mentioned terrorist groups is evidence of the paradoxical phenomenon that while the Pakistani government and the Pakistani Taliban are bitter enemies, at the same time there has been collusion between the Inter-Services Intelligence (ISI) and jihadists in the Taliban and many related jihadist groups who have been used as to promote the policies of the Pakistani government. The LeT in particular has been used extensively by the ISI as proxy fighters in Kashmir operations. For this reason, persons can be at risk both from terrorists, and from the government's intelligence services and other security services. In particular, it is in accordance with the objective evidence discussed above that political activists on Kashmir will be at risk from Jama'at-ud-Da'awa and Hizb-ul-Mujahedeen.

It is clear that the Hizb-ul-Mujahedeen seeks to replace the JKFL in Jammu and Kashmir and therefore members and supporters of the JFKL are at risk from this group, as are members of the UKPNP. According to the India Times,"HuM ... tried to eliminate JKLF cadre by providing in intelligence to security forces and even killed JFKL men themselves in clashes. Nearly 300 JFKL cadre were killed by HuM.[98]

2.4 The possibility of protection and relocation in Pakistan

In asylum cases, the question of protection against the risks from political violence and the viability of relocation inside the country is a critical issue. The authorities routinely assert that protection is available, and the relocation is possible. For victims of political violence, however, there is often no possibility that the asylum applicant could receive any credible protection either from the police or the military in Pakistan, especially if the latter are seeking to persecute him or her. Relocation within the country will not mitigate the risks as will be discussed in more detail below.

Although it is sometimes claimed that there are "avenues of redress" against the Taliban or other militants from the police in Pakistan, the objective evidence indicates that this does not conform to the reality on the ground in Pakistan. In the understanding of Western countries, the role of the police is to protect the public against criminals and security threats. In Pakistan, the police do not play this role and the general public consider the police a source of threat. The police are perceived to be incompetent, inadequate, unresponsive to requests for help and engaged in an institutionalised abuse of power as well as thoroughly corrupt. Policing by consent does not really exist. Ordinary citizens do not co-operate with the police, they do not see the police as an instrument of the rule of law, but as a politicized force serving the needs of the powerful.[99] The UK authorities are aware of this issue, and they like to make reference to recent reforms, but these are irrelevant because their effect so marginal that it has no consequence. A close analysis of the claim that there is sufficiency of protection in Pakistan shows there is no substance to it because it amounts to saying that protection is available because a police force does exist, without examining closely the behaviour and the effectiveness of the police force (or rather the lack of it).

Public attitudes to the police in Pakistan are a result of every-day experience of a force that ordinary people see as operation outside the bounds of a civilised code of behaviour. This conduct has so far been impervious to efforts by some politicians to change it and any recent improvements, any reforms have been very partial and not affected the fundamental patterns of police behaviour. Any arrangements for citizens to challenge police misconduct, to seek redress against injustice are inadequate and ineffective. There is no public confidence in the police, and for good reason.[100]

According to a Human Rights Watch Report the police in Pakistan is both corrupt and elite members of society in Pakistan exercise undue control over the law enforcement authorities: "Public surveys and reports of government accountability and redress institutions show that the police are one of the most widely feared, complained against, and least trusted government institutions in Pakistan, lacking a clear system of accountability and plagued by corruption at the highest levels. District-level police are often under the control of powerful politicians, wealthy landowners, and other influential members of society. There are numerous reported cases of police extrajudicial killings of criminal suspects, torture of detainees to obtain confessions, and harassment and extortion of individuals who seek to file criminal cases, especially against members of the security forces." "Pakistani police also use their extensive powers of registration of cases, arrest, and detention at the behest of powerful societal elites (the wealthy, politicians, landowners, and civil and military bureaucracy) to bring false charges against perceived opponents as a form of intimidation or punishment." "Elite elements within Pakistani society – be they politicians, landowners, or members of civil and military bureaucracy – exercise outsized and improper control over law enforcement."[101]

Human Rights Watch have summarised the conclusions of their report as follows: "This report documents custodial torture, extrajudicial executions, and other serious human rights violations by the police in Pakistan. It details the difficulties that victims of crime and police abuse face in obtaining justice, including the refusal by police to register complaints (known as First Information Reports or FIRs), their demands for bribes, and biased investigations. The poor and other vulnerable or marginalized groups invariably face the greatest obstacles to obtaining justice in a system that is rigged against them. It also examines limitations, including financial and human resource constraints, which police say impact their ability to function properly, and looks at examples of some good police practices that can serve as possible models for the future... The corruption and abuse endemic to the Pakistani law enforcement system are often described as "*thana* culture," after the Urdu word for police station. Many police officers told Human Rights Watch that abuses can often be explained, if not justified, by the considerable pressures placed upon them. They listed organizational shortcomings, inadequate training and resources, lack of requisite funds, poor working conditions, and lack of coordination with other law enforcement agencies as obstacles to transparency and accountability within the police force. All of these problems, they said, were exacerbated by pressures imposed by senior police officials to achieve results, and by politicians and other local elites with their own agendas."[102]

It is a common belief among Pakistani people that the police could not protect them against criminals, the Taliban or other militants.[103] The ineffectiveness of the police, the level of corruption and the mistreatment they often accord to ordinary people is confirmed by the objective evidence. The police can often not be relied upon to deal with ordinary crime. This is in line with a recent study of the respected International Crisis Group which concluded: "Pakistan's police force is incapable of combating crime, upholding the law or protecting citizens and the state against militant violence."[104] Ordinary people would avoid contacting the police about even minor problems, because they would usually expect to have to pay a bribe. The police always convey the presumption that anyone dealing with them has done something wrong, hence the need to pay money. In worse cases individuals can be arrested.[105] The inability of the police in Pakistan to combat crime, never mind terrorism, has been thoroughly documented in a report by the International Crisis Group.[106] Anatol Lieven cites police officers in

Punjab who rely on beating and torturing suspects and prefer this to the use of modern forensic methods, and comments that together with "the general police tendency to take bribes in return for every service, it is hardly surprising therefore that people avoid the police as much as possible…"[107]. Corruption is pervasive in Pakistan, and affects the police in particular. Thus the Financial Daily, in a recent report on corruption in Pakistan, stated: "As regards the police, they work in collaboration with street criminals, gangs, criminals. Those who went against these gangs either lost their life, or were forced to leave the force."[108]

The police are not trained or equipped to provide protection to the general public against criminal gangs or militants. Lack of resources (including equipment) and low levels of pay are demoralising. Anatol Lieven cites a police officer from the Khyber Pakhtunkhwa: "We need better accommodation – look at this place. We need better vehicles, better radios, better arms, bullet-proof vests, Tell me, could any police force in the world work well given what we have to rely on? Would you risk your life fighting the Taliban for the pay we get?"[109] There have been various attacks on police and police facilities in Punjab. These have revealed that the police are usually outgunned by the extremists. Efforts to arrest individuals are hampered by the reluctance of the police to act. For example, when they attempted to arrest a commander of the banned group Jaish-e-Mohammed in a hospital in Bahawalpur, they were threatened with attacks on police stations and the police backed down rather than confront the militants.[110] No person in Pakistan having been issued by death threats from Taliban would rely on the police to protect them.[111]

A Country Risk assessment from Jane's states that the police force has become steadily politicized over the years and that corruption is rife in the service.[112] The report refers to public perception surveys according to which the police is "the most corrupt of all services" It also states that "investigative procedures are generally brutal and frequently consist of torturing a suspect until a confession is obtained". This was confirmed by a study on prisons showing that 91.54 percent of detained men and 8.46 percent detained women are victims of physical torture by the police.[113] Torture techniques involved rolling heavy objects over the prisoners, jumping on them, placing them on ice blocks, hanging them by their arms, hitting people with hammers and hanging them upside down. Reports indicate that prisoners are tortured in order to obtain confessions, obviating the need for further criminal investigation.[114] According to the British charity Reprieve, people are arrested and physically tortured without any physical evidence against them.[115] According to Amnesty International, more than 100 persons die every year in police custody.[116]

Despite various reports of reforms, the situation has not fundamentally changed. Thus a report in 2018 confirmed: "According to the latest surveys, the police force is considered as the most corrupt institution of Pakistan."[117] Likewise it was reported: "Public surveys and reports of government accountability and redress institutions show that the police are one of the most widely feared, complained against, and least trusted government institutions in Pakistan, lacking a clear system of accountability and plagued by corruption at the highest levels. District-level police are often under the control of powerful politicians, wealthy landowners, and other influential members of society. There are numerous reported cases of police extrajudicial killings of criminal suspects, torture of detainees to obtain confessions, and harassment and extortion of individuals who seek to file criminal cases, especially against members of the security forces."[118] While mechanisms to complain against treatment by the authorities technically exist, they are completely ineffective and ordinary people cannot count on getting redress of mistreatment by the police or rely on police protection against sectarian and extremist threats. In view of the fact that this behaviour by the police is common knowledge, it is understandable that ordinary people will avoid contact with the police, especially if they are from an area known to harbour militants, as they fear arrest and mistreatment.

Although the Pakistani judicial system is substantially based on the legal system inherited from the British, it does not function as it is does in the United Kingdom because of endemic corruption, the conflict with customary laws and a completely different understanding of the purpose of the judicial system. In the United Kingdom the judicial system protects the rights of the individual and sanctions offenders. In Pakistan, the purpose of the judicial system is to mediate political conflicts and maintain social stability. The individual is subject to the state law, the law of religion (the Shariah) and local community or tribal law. Authorities who administer state law also have to abide by shariah law and often accept the observance of community law which can mean turning a blind eye to criminal behaviour (under state law) and violence (including murder).[119] The problem in cases involving members of the UKPNP or similar pro-Kashmir independence groups is that the authorities will seek to persecute rather than protect them. Interaction with the authorities will result in criminal investigations against them.

Although the UK authorities claim that because Pakistan is quite a large country it would be possible for persons at risk from terrorists or other forms of political violence to relocate within Pakistan, this ignores the existence of the National Database and Registration Authority in Pakistan The authorities or someone with connections with the security services could access the NADRA national database and locate the any person.[120] Every person who seeks employment, to engage in business or to rent or buy property needs to present an ID card with a NADRA identification code.[121] Anyone in the police or with connections to the police would also be able to access the NADRA system. The Home Office is aware of this issue which has been frequently brought to their attention, but to my knowledge it has never engaged with it and continues to assert that it is possible for people to "disappear" in Pakistan as far as the persons who seek to harm them is concerned. The evidence to the contrary is simply ignored.

Another issue is whether the Pakistani authorities are aware about the activities of opponents of the government, including UKPNP members, in the United Kingdom. The ISI is charged with foreign and domestic intelligence. Its domestic political activities range from managing to supressing political opposition. A significant aspect of its role is the surveillance of its cadre, foreigners, the media, foreign diplomats accredited to Pakistan, Pakistani diplomats serving outside the country, dissidents abroad and the interception and monitoring of communications. The ISI monitors the activities of the UKPNP abroad. The ISI operations in the United Kingdom have been described as "the most comprehensive outside Pakistan", using support from the 1.2 million strong Pakistani community in the UK.[122]

The advancement of Pakistan's position on Kashmir and to counter opposition to it is one of the principal missions of the ISI in the UK.[123] It has also been revealed that the ISI monitors communication of its citizens to Pakistan.[124] The UK authorities live in a strange state of denial. It must be presumed that other sections of the UK government are fully aware of ISI operations in the UK, but the Home Office continues to deny their existence.

2.5 Feudalism and Land conflicts in Pakistan

According to an academic study, "Feudalism is a system of receiving land from a king and in return working and fighting for him. Feudalism is also defined by a system of landownership by superior classes in special relation to the royal or state power. A feudal had to collect tax whether in coin or in kind on the behalf of the state and deposit it in the royal exchequer. Moreover, a feudal had to cultivate an army which could help the state whenever required. A feudal was answerable to the central authority and not to the peasants or to the members of the villages inhabiting his fief. The Sultans of Delhi, the Mughals and the British, who invaded, occupied and ruled over the subcontinent, promoted feudalism in the subcontinent to hold their foot on it."[125]

Contemporary Pakistan is still dealing with the legacy of feudalism which it inherited from the colonial era and which is manifest in the power and influence of large landowning families that control enormous estates, especially in the more remote areas. Feudalism in Pakistan refers to a group of powerful and politically landowners, who believe that they are entitled to their property and political influences. Around five per cent of households in the countryside own about two thirds of Pakistani agricultural land. The owners of thousands of acres of land exercise their power through debt bondage and control over the distribution of water, fertilisers, agricultural credits and tractor permits. They exercise control over the income, the judicial administration and the police nominally subject to the local government. The large landlord families also influence government affairs at the national level, they influence the government bureaucracy and the entire political class. The large majority of the members of the

National Assembly and key executive posts in the provinces are held by members of the feudal elite of the country.[126]

According to the academic study cited above, "In Pakistan, the feudal are known as Chaudharies, Warraich, Pirs, Khans, Makhdooms, Arbabs, Mizaris, Khars, Legharis, Nawabzadas, Nawabs, Sardars and Shahs. No province of Pakistan is immune to feudalism whether it exists in the form of Zamindars, tribal chiefs or Pirs. The outward manifestations of feudalism are big lands, peasants and private jails in rural areas and spacious houses and luxurious life style in urban areas."[127]

Almost half of Pakistan's economy and most of its export earnings depend on the agricultural sector. The countryside is controlled by several thousand feudal families. This concentration of economic power translates into political power and the Pakistan Muslim League that established Pakistan in 1947 was dominated by feudal landowners. For example, the Bhutto family that played such a dominant role in the history of Pakistan is a large family of landowners from Sindh, represented more recently by the former President Zardari.[128]

Although the development of the Pakistani state with the dominant role of the military, industrialization and the growing importance of financial capital have weakened the importance of feudalism, it remains a strong force inside the country. This means that local authorities in the Pakistani countryside in particular, including the police and the courts, will not support ordinary workers and peasants against the powerful landlords whose edict prevails.

The caste system in South Asia has a long history and various forms and especially known among Hindus in India where a caste system was defined on the basis of "verma" or colour, later modified by classification based on profession. Pakistanis share the same cultural roots and accepted the caste system is based on "jati," or birth. There are no castes in Islam but local Muslim societies in South Asia adopted the existing societal stratification in the region.[129]

Looking at the case system in terms of occupation and profession, the following stratification can be observed: "Zamindar, or landowner, is the highest; then lohar-thrukkhan, or blacksmith-carpenter; then poly, or weaver; mochi, or cobbler; meerasi-naie, or entertainer-barber.

In Pakistan, the equivalents of Hindu untouchables are chammar, chura and bhangi, or janitor. These people have separate plates and cups in all employee cafeterias. They are mainly Christian, although some are Hindus and Muslims. The caste system, in its feudal origins, reflected the importance of professions and occupations for agricultural output. Blacksmith-carpenters were important because they produced tools for agriculture, thus their high status. Pakistan is predominantly an underdeveloped agricultural society. While the caste system has religious approval under Hinduism, it has no future in an industrializing Muslim society. In an industrial era, castes are replaced by classes."[130]

Thus, the caste system reflects the hierarchy of power in society: "The landowners are followed by comparatively "lower" castes including *lohar, tarkhan, mochi, mirasi* who are then followed by *chooray, chamar and masalis.* Keeping the lower castes aside, even the middle and the upper middle classes have divided themselves into a number of castes including *Rajput, Syed, Dhillon, Butt, Bhattis, Jutt, Janjua, Siqqiquis* and many more which cannot be mentioned because the list will never end."Lower castes" are referred to as *Neech Zaat* (low caste) and *Badnasal* (of bad lineage). In **Balochistan** the "lower castes" include *Ghulams* (slaves), *Lohris* (musicians), and *Lachhis* (Dalits). In Sindh, "high-caste" Muslims, in addition to *Shahs* and *Syeds*, include the *Akhunds, Effendis, Soomros, Talpurs,* and *Pirs. Hajjams* (barbers), *Dhobis* (washers), *Kumbhars* (potters), *Maachis/ Mallahs*(fisherfolk) and *Bhajeer* (Dalit converts to Islam) are considered "low caste".[131]

Feudalism and the caste system are in an interacting informal system of a hierarchy of power in Pakistan that involves privilege versus discrimination, that results in millions of low caste persons who do not own land subsisting in what some call slavery, or debt bondage, or serfdom.[132] The way in Pakistani society functions, those in lower castes and without property can expect fair treatment from the authorities and the governmental institutions against the power of those in the upper castes and those in the land-owning classes.

Land disputes in Pakistan are quite common. The ownership of land (freehold property) is typically held by extended families and the eldest member of the family or head of the household is deemed to hold the title. The complexity and costs of the process of formally registering titles has led to the failure of many families to formally register the ownership of land. This results in complications in relation to enforcing property rights through the courts.[133]

The Pakistani government has acknowledged that there are many problematic features of the land revenue system, the complexity of the procedures and the dispersed and duplicative nature of the land records renders land rights uncertain and affects in particular the vulnerable and poor whose rights remain in practice unprotected. In Punjab, for example, it has been note that "...high transaction costs and difficulties associated with the land records system continue to impose significant harm on land owners and prospective land owners, (particularly the poor, who have small holdings and less access to information or resources), making them vulnerable to the predatory behaviour of middlemen, and lowering the liquidity of family assets composed in whole or in part of land. As land is also a form of capital, current obstacles for documenting and enforcing land rights have the effect of lowering income from those assets through means such as rent, cultivation, sale, or access to other factors (e.g. credit)."[134]

Usually families place a high priority on keeping their land in the family and if the eldest dies, the rest of the family inherits the land with the eldest formally retaining ownership. One of the reasons why it is so common in Pakistan for women to marry their cousins through arranged marriages is that in this way the land remains in the family.

The common also of land disputes has also given rise to violence and killings in private land disputes have become very common. According to the Pakistani newspaper *Dawn*, land disputes have become the most common motive for murder in the Pakistani capital Islamabad: "Land and property disputes leave all other motives for murder far behind in the federal capital. In the past, such disputes used to be prevalent in rural areas, but the growing trend of urbanisation has brought it to the peripheries of big cities where price of real estate has been rising fast. Since Islamabad is the choicest place for many, particularly the moneyed class, to live in or invest, land here fetches the highest price."[135] Records of killings in land dispute go back to the 1940s to the time before partition when four people were burned alive due to a land dispute.

Recent cases include a dispute involved two cousins - Haji Nawaz Khokhar and Abdul Rasheed - over a piece of land measuring about 10 kanals in Alipur Farash. This family conflicted claimed eight lives within four years, all due to revenge killings resulting from enmity over the piece of land. Now only two men are alive in the family of Abdul Rasheed. All others have been killed as a result this feud over land. In the period from February 2006 to July 2007, the bitter dispute claimed seven lives. Both sides were warned on a number of occasions by the police, but the killings continued and were not prevented by the police. More recently, on 9 March 2010, another family member of Abdul Rasheed was shot dead by unidentified persons. This is one of myriad examples where private land disputes within a family turned deadly, were carried on over a period of many years and the police proved completely unable to prevent further killings.[136]

Other recent examples of the kind of violence that occurs in Pakistan in land feuds have been reported. In Jamrud Thesil of Khyber agency three members of a family were killed in a land dispute in 2013.[137] On 28 August 2013 it was reported that at least four persons were killed and another injured in an armed clash between two rival groups over a land dispute here in Gujranwala. Armed men of two groups from village Wahendo, tehsil Kamonki of Gujranwala district engaged in a shooting battle because of an old rivalry over the ownership of a piece of land. Four people were killed, and another was wounded.[138]

To summarize, disputes involving land that become violent are quite common in Pakistan. There is also evidence that parties to a land dispute are still pursuing potential rivals after many years and are willing to go to substantial lengths to find and kill them.[139]

CHAPTER 3

Violence related to family honour in Pakistan

3.1 Domestic Violence and honour killings in Pakistan

In Pakistan, as in many other countries, domestic violence is a pervasive and persistent problem. Academic studies found that the number of women suffering domestic abuse in Pakistan is around 70%, and one academic survey reported in found that 96.76% of the women questioned reported that they had been seriously abused.[140] Every year about 5000 women in Pakistan are killed as a result of domestic violence, any many other thousands are maimed or disabled. Sexual abuse, The Thomson Foundation issued a study according to with Pakistan was ranked as the third most dangerous country in the world for women, after Afghanistan and the Democratic Republic of Congo.[141] Most victims have no legal recourse and are unable to receive police protection. This is a consequence of the fact that the police and other authorities do not view domestic violence as a crime and will decline to register cases brought before them. Given the scale of the problem and the low number of shelters in for women, the acceptance of abuse in families means it is almost impossible for victims to escape from violent home environments.

An academic study on violence against women in Pakistan stated: "Male dominance is frequently mentioned as a determinant of the domestic violence. Decision making authority makes the man more dominant in the family and society and increases the likelihood against women. Pakistani society is a patriarchal society in which, male members who bear the decision-making authority, head the families. Women are usually not included in making decisions and are considered socially and economically dependent on men. Women consider themselves insecure, incomplete, ineffective and inefficient without males."[142]

It is common in Pakistan for parents whose daughters or sons marry without their consent or against their wishes, or for husbands whose wives seek to leave them, to consider these actions to seriously damage the honour of the family, with many resorting to killing the offending person. Honour killings can be carried out by in-laws against a woman who separates from or divorces her husband, or by the husband himself, by her brothers if they think she has dishonoured the family by lewd behaviour (including rejecting an arranged marriage), or her parents and other relatives. In addition to matters of honour (sexual conduct, having been raped, choice of marriage partner, divorce) honour killings are often motivated by efforts to preserve family assets (this one reason why families often insist that a woman marries a cousin), acquire the assets of another family or enhance the reputation and influence of the family.[143]

It is important to consider the risks faced by Pakistani women in particular whose families believe that they violated the family's honour. Among the "violations of honour" are rejecting an arranged marriage, entering an unapproved marriage or even worse, sexual activity outside marriage. Many women and men who have been accused of such "violations" have become the target of an honour killing. In Pakistan, women and men are usually expected to accept an arranged marriage with someone from their own clan and family, and marriage to someone from a different clan, caste and social background is highly disapproved of, potentially to the point of provoking attempts to kill the person involved. The husband and the wife can become the target of attack or honour killing.

It is common in Pakistan for parents whose daughters or sons marry without their consent or against their wishes to consider these actions to seriously damage the honour of the family, with many resorting to killing the offending person. Honour killings can be carried out by parents, brothers or other relatives against a woman or man who is in an unapproved relationship or if they think she has dishonoured the family by lewd behaviour (including rejecting an arranged marriage). In addition to matters of honour (sexual conduct, having been raped, choice of marriage partner, divorce) honour killings are often motivated by efforts to preserve family assets (this one reason why families often insist that a woman marries a cousin), acquire the assets of another family or covering up other crimes.[144] Often families are preoccupied with safeguarding their property against other families and insist on marriage within the family as a result. Marriages arranged between cousins are exceedingly common in Pakistan, and marriage outside the family and especially outside the clan is strongly disapproved of and can provoke violent reactions against the couple involved. In many cases men offended against the family of a girlfriend by having a clandestine and unapproved relationship.

The truth is that millions of women in Pakistan live in mortal fear. If they are suspected of having brought shame on the family they can be killed by shooting, burning or killing with axes. The tradition of honour is associated with the understanding of the role of man as the head of the household in which women are effectively understood as the property of men, obliged to obey their every whim. These concepts so deeply entrenched in the social, political and economic fabric of Pakistan that the government is unable to prevent the enslavement, killing and maiming of individuals by their families. Islamic leaders provide religious justification for sanctioning honour killings.[145] While honour killings affecting women have attracted most attention, insulting the honour of a family can be justification for violence against husbands, fathers and other men involved. As a recent report noted: "Another important thing to note is that crimes of honour are not gender restricted. Men can also be victimised by the family members of the woman with whom they are perceived to be romantically involved. Although honour crimes more often target women, they are in no way limited to women alone."[146]

Many cases of honour killings have been documented. For example, Taslim Khatoon Solangi, 17, of Hajna Shah village in Khairpur district, was eight months pregnant. She was tortured and killed on 7 March 2005 at the behest of her father-in-law on the grounds that she allegedly carried a child conceived outside of marriage.[147] Another case concerns three teenage girls who were buried alive because they refused to enter arranged marriages.[148] On 6 January 1999 a woman called Ghazala living in Joharabad, Punjab province, was set on fire by her brother. Her family killed her because they suspected her of having an "illicit" relationship with a neighbour. More recently, a married couple was killed by their family for entering the marriage without consent, having been lured into returning home under false pretences. According to the press report, "Muafia Bibi, 17, and her husband, Sajjad Ahmed, 30, were drugged and their throats were slit in Satrah on Friday night, allegedly by the girl's family, police said. Asghar Ali, the local police chief, said Bibi's parents and three other family members convinced the recently married couple to return to the family home by saying they approved of the marriage."[149] This just a small sample of thousands of similar cases. In the last two years there has been a surge of honour killings in Pakistan.[150] Most recently the killing of a Pakistani celebrity Qandeel Balouch by her own brother because her behaviour allegedly brought shame on the family has been reported.[151]

In the United Kingdom there are numerous women in safe houses provided for by social services who have been attacked or threatened by their husbands or other relatives.[152] For example, on one occasion I encountered three Pakistani women who were living in such accommodation in Bradford. One was being stalked by her ex-husband, a cousin she was forced to marry in Pakistan and whom she divorced because he refused to permit her to continue her education. The documents submitted for the divorce stated that her husband had raped her six times. The husband sought to persuade the then UK Border Agency to have her deported to Pakistan, so that she could be killed with impunity. A second woman had been run over by her husband in his Mercedes and her leg was in a cast. The third lady had received serious threats from her in-laws. The key relevance to the current case is that in Pakistan people believe that they can kill their enemies with impunity, in particular if they make the argument that somehow the honour of their family was injured.

In Pakistan honour killings, known as karo-kari in Sindh province and kala/kali in Punjab, often find support in Pakistani society, especially in rural areas. It is estimated that there are more than 10,000 honour killings in Pakistan every year.[153] The concepts of honour are very deeply entrenched in the culture of the country, and the authorities mostly ignore the killing or maiming of women and men by their families. If the perpetrators are prosecuted the sentences are often light in relation to the offense. Thus, an Amnesty International report condemned "the failure of the authorities to prevent these killings by investigating and punishing the perpetrators."[154] According to a recent study: "The attitudes demonstrated by the police and judges reflect the overwhelming social acceptance of honour crimes, the influence of power holders and the absence of rule of law. Policemen are part of Pakistani society in which women are not held in very high regard."[155] The method and circumstances of killing vary in different provinces. In Punjab killings are often carried out by shooting in secret by individuals (usually husbands, fathers or brothers). In Sindh the targets are often hacked to pieces with the consent of the community. Tribal councils (*jirgas*) sometimes rule that a woman should be killed and dispatch men to carry out this deed; likewise, they order the killing of men in cases of honour or other alleged crimes. The whole of Pakistan is divided into tribes, clans and families and *jirgas* operate everywhere in parallel to the state criminal justice system.

Honour killings mostly go unreported and most of them go unpunished. The police usually take the side of the men who perpetrate these acts and killers are rarely prosecuted. Even in the rare case when a man is convicted, he is likely to receive a light sentence. The Women's Protection Act of 2006 brought the crime of rape under the jurisdiction of criminal courts rather than Islamic courts where a woman was required to produce four male witnesses to corroborate the charge. These facts, however, do not change the realities on the ground in relation to honour killings which according to many reports have continued unabated.

Honour killings have long been crimes under Pakistan's criminal code. But there has been a systematic failure by the state to end honour killings, to investigate them and hold the perpetrators to account. Successive Pakistani governments have failed to engage in sustained and serious efforts to overcome culturally conditioned attitudes to such crimes as honour killings and rape. In recent years women in Pakistan have been willing to come forward more often to report the threats against them, and cases of honour killings are more frequently reported.

The Criminal Law (Amendment) Act 2004, for the first time, 'honour' crimes were defined in the Pakistan Penal Code. The Act requires that crimes committed under the pretext of honour attract a set of punishments, and in particular murder justified by "honour" has to be punished, although there is considerable discretion in sentencing that ranges from ten years in prison to capital punishment.[156]

However the provisions against "honour crimes" in the penal code are routinely circumvented, as a study reports: "From the perspective of prosecution, the fact that legal heirs of a victim still retain the right of dropping charges at any point during the trial entails a risk that all the effort involved in investigation and collection of evidence can be in vain. It has also been reported that the First Investigation Reports (FIRs) fail to record honour killings under the relevant provisions of the Penal Code as amended by the Criminal Law (Amendment) Act, 2004 as a result of collusion between the accused and the police." The research shows that the words honour killing are never actually used. In this way any positive aspect of the 2004 legislation is avoided, in particular the restrictions on compromise between the victim's family and the perpetrator which may allow the perpetrator to escape any serious punishment altogether. The research "based on an analysis of FIRs and interviews with lawyers and victims' families in four districts (Naseerabad, Ghotki, Nowshera, and Gujrat), puts the practice down partly to the collusion between the accused and the police in exchange for bribes... Despite express provisions to the contrary, the culture of out-of-court settlements still runs deep, and the police are known to encourage the practice."[157]

There is a large body of anecdotal evidence as well as academic studies showing that sufficiency of protection is not available in Pakistan for persons who are targets of honour killings. It is common knowledge in Pakistan that the police cannot be relied upon to side with and support the victims of efforts to kill them in the name of honour. Indeed, given the prevailing attitude towards honour killings and the general culture of corruption of the police, individuals would not be wise to rely on this idea. In addition to women, the husbands whose wives are deemed to have insulted the honour of their families by the unapproved marriage are also subject to attack or even murder, and honour killings can affect anyone who is deemed to have offended against the honour of someone.

In relation to violence against women, the attitude of the police and judiciary in general is that these are family matters. According to a report by the Asia Society:

Women face a form of violence in their interactions with law enforcement agencies as complainants. This "structural violence" manifests itself in the form of insensitivity within the justice system toward female complainants, negligence in responding, delay in action, and outright refusal to recognize the occurrence of violence. The behaviour of the police toward women in Pakistan reflects the general attitude of Pakistani society as a whole, which is intent on denying the existence of violence and sending women back to their homes in the custody of a male guardian. If a woman seeks justice, she first has to register a case – through as a First Information Report (FIR) – with the police. Even before doing so, she is immediately viewed as suspect, as it is generally believed that no decent woman would venture into a police station. If the case involves a family member, the police will brush it aside as a private matter to be resolved at home. Bribery, extortion, and coercion are all used to discourage or falsify registration."[158]

According to a report by the US State Department, "NGOs reported police were at times implicated in rape cases. NGOs also alleged police sometimes abused or threatened victims, demanding they drop charges, especially when police received bribes from suspected perpetrators. Some police demanded bribes from victims before registering rape charges, and investigations were sometimes superficial. While the use of post-rape medical testing increased during the year, medical personnel in many areas did not have sufficient training or equipment, which further complicated prosecutions."[159]

Women are right to believe that she cannot seek protection from the police, and this conforms to the perception of the general public in Pakistan of the police and the reality of the experiences that ordinary people have. Although the Pakistani judicial system is substantially based on the legal system inherited from the British, it does not function as it is does in the United Kingdom because of endemic corruption, the conflict with customary laws and a completely different understanding of the purpose of the judicial system. In the United Kingdom the judicial system protects the rights of the individual and sanctions offenders. In Pakistan, the purpose of the judicial system is to mediate political conflicts and maintain social stability. The individual is subject to the state law, the law of religion (the Shariah) and local community or tribal law. Authorities who administer state law also have to abide by shariah law and often accept the observance of community law which can mean turning a blind eye to criminal behaviour (under state law) and violence (including murder).[160]

3.2 Persecution for sexual offences ("zina")

While in relation to honour crimes the most serious criticism of the authorities is the failure to protect the victims and apply the criminal code properly, there is a more sinister abuse of law whereby the state itself can be instrumentalised to engage in persecution on behalf of the perpetrators, and that is the use of the ordinances in relation to "zina" (adultery or fornication).

One way in which *zina* is punished is outside the judicial system. The whole of Pakistan is divided into tribes, clans and families and *jirgas* operate everywhere in parallel to the state criminal justice system. They often issue very severe judgements. For example, they can rule that a woman should be killed and dispatch men to carry out this deed; likewise they order the killing of men in cases of honour or other alleged crimes.

There are many cases in reported in which jirgas (or "panchayat") mete out serious punishments to those who are deemed to be involved in "zina" (adultery or fornication) or other violations of honour. In May 2016 it was reported that a 16-year old girl "Ambreen Riasat, who was drugged, killed and burned by a group of men in a so-called "honour killing" in the village of Makol, just 50 km from the capital Islamabad".[161] Her alleged crime was that she helped a couple in an unapproved relationship to elope.

A report by IRIN ("Integrated Regional Information Networks) highlighted the power of the jirgas, especially in the Federally Administered Tribal Areas and the Khyber Pakhtunkhwa: "... women in KP were "frequently produced before jirgas", most often in cases of ʿswaraʾ or "marriages of exchange", where they were handed over to an aggrieved party to settle a dispute, including murder or other crime. "Under-age girls are often produced before jirgas by their fathers in such cases," Minallah said. The ʿjirgasʾ often help reinforce discrimination against women, which can be particularly acute in rural areas in the north. In the remote Kohistan District of KP where, technically speaking at least, national law applies, three men were shot dead in January this year as a result of a long-standing tribal feud involving allegations their brothers had mingled with unrelated women. «In Kohistan, the ease with which people are willing to kill women, often on ʿjirgaʾ orders, is shocking. It is just something completely acceptable to them,» said Farzana Bari, chairperson of the Womenʾs Study Centre at Quaid-e-Azam University in Islamabad and a well-known womenʾs rights activist who headed a Supreme Court inquiry into the case."[162]

But the threat to individuals does not only come from efforts by the members of a jirga to mete out the punishment if the target individual returns to Pakistan, but also from the authorities in Pakistan if a charge of "zina" were to be brought against her (or him).

In 1979 the then President of Pakistan General Zia Ul Haq introduced a set of laws known as the "Hudood Ordinances". This was part of an effort to turn Pakistan into an Islamic country and the laws were designed to bring the criminal justice system more in line with certain injunctions in Islam. It relates to offences punishable by *hadd*, i.e. ordained by the Holy Quran. The Offence of Zina (Enforcement of Hudood) Ordinance (Zina Ordinance) repealed almost all sections of the Pakistan Penal Code, which had governed sexual offenses including rape, and replaced them with its own ostensibly Islamic provisions. All sexual intercourse outside marriage became a criminal offense. An offense of unlawful sexual intercourse (Zina) takes place wherever "a man and a woman ... wilfully have sexual intercourse without being validly married to each other" (Section 4 of the Zina ordinance).[163]

In addition to the offence of Zina, the Hudood Ordinances also defined the offense of Qazf (wrongful accusation of Zina crimes), and offences Against Property and Prohibition. The manner in which these ordinances were applied gave rise to much criticism, because of the ambiguity in the concepts of Zina (adultery or other unlawful sex) and rape (Zina bil Jabr). The accusation of rape was hard to prove, as it required four male eyewitnesses to be sustained. If the court did not accept that rape had been proven, the woman would automatically be assumed to be guilty of Zina, which could lead to very harsh punishment (including the death penalty if she was married). Moreover, it is very common that husbands accuse their wives of Zina, especially if they want to end the relationship and have themselves committed this offence. Pregnancy alleged to be "extramarital" has been a common way for husbands to prove their wife's "Zina", because it does not require any further corroborating evidence. The criminal justice system has generally favoured the husbands and women have found it hard to get a hearing either with the police or the courts, and thousands of women have been arrested and incarcerated after suspicions of Zina were raised.[164]

On 15 November 2006 the Pakistani National Assembly passed the Women's Protection Act (WPA) at the behest of then President Pervez Musharraf. The purpose of this legislation was to address some of the issues relating to the Hudood ordinances which had been heavily criticized at home and abroad. The act incorporated some of the offences from the *Hudood ordinances* relating to Zina and incorporated them in the Pakistan Penal Code. The act defined new offences of fornication and false accusation of fornication with the intention that these would replace the relevant sections in the Hudood Ordinances. Instead of "Hadood Offences", "fornication" and "rape" would become "ta'zir offences" to be dealt with by Pakistan's Criminal Code.[165]

Although supporters of women's rights widely welcomed the WPA, observers were sceptical about the practical effect of the act. The most important reason is that the Hadood Ordinances reflected widespread cultural practices and beliefs both in the general population and the criminal justice system, and the evidence that has accumulated since then bears out the suspicion that little has changed in practice. Part of this scepticism is due to the fact that much of the text defining the new offences in the Criminal Code were taken straight from the text of the Hadood Ordinances. Adultery and similar sexual offences are still criminal offences and could be punished more harshly even than under the Hadood Ordinances. Fornication will be punished with at least five years imprisonment. The only tangible difference is that it is no longer possible that an allegation of rape is converted into an allegation of zina (fornication), and there are harsh penalties for false allegations of fornication.[166]

The WPA also created new procedures for the prosecution of fornication, adultery and related offences. According to section 203C of the Criminal Procedure Code, a complaint of fornication can only be lodged in the court of a magistrate first class. This procedure is supposed to replace that of lodging a First Information Report (FIR) with the police. This makes it more difficult to pursue such allegations and has the paradoxical effect of making it more difficult for poor women to pursue allegations of rape. Another issue with the WPA is that it does not apply to the FATA (federally administered tribal areas) or the PATA (provincially Administered Tribal Areas) and prosecutions under the Hudood Ordinances can still be brought.[167]

The practical effects of these changes remain limited. Although some women were released from prison, others remained incarcerated. A survey showed that two years after its passage police stations did not have copies of the WPA and were unaware of its meaning. There seems to have been no let-up in the registration of FIRs in relation to Zina type offences since the WPA came into effect.[168] The idea that a change in the laws would suddenly override previous practice is in conformity with the British understanding of criminal justice but not in accordance with the cultural norms that define criminal justice in Pakistan. It should be noted that those accused of *zina* commonly have FIRs lodged against them that accuse of common crimes such as the theft, although it mentions that the offence of Zina has been committed and that a complaint has been filed at the session court, in order to provide a simpler route to prosecution.

The role of the Federal Shariat Court muddies the waters even further. The role of the FSC is to determine whether the laws of Pakistan are in compliance with Shari'a law. The FSC also exercises revisional jurisdiction of the criminal courts in relation to Hadood cases. The decisions of the FSC are binding on the High Courts and lower courts. Although the intention of the WPA is to remove Zina-related cases from the Hadood ordinances, the status of such offenses remained ambiguous given the widespread consensus among Muslim scholars that sexual offenses are governed by the Shari 'a, they do constitute Hadood offenses and there are subject to the jurisdiction of the FSC.[169]

The Federal Shariat Court took a major step in 2010 to resolve this conflict. In its consideration of the various provision of the WPA, On 22 December 2010, the Federal Shariat Court (FSC) declared three sections of the 2006 Women's Protection Act void, on the basis that the provisions violate Section 203DD of Pakistan's Constitution. THE FSC was exercising its power to review the finding of any criminal court under any law relating to the enforcement of Hudood. According to the Daily Times the FSC decision:

"seeks to restore the primacy of Hudood laws in cases relating to the offence of *zina* (adultery) and *qazaf* (false accusation of adultery), which have a long history of abuse and injustice. The Women's Protection Act 2006 omitted two sections of the Hudood Ordinances which, to some extent, reduced the likelihood of abuse of these laws against women accused of adultery. Their cases could now be tried under the Pakistan Penal Code, instead of exclusively under the Hudood Ordinance. However, not only did the FSC declare Sections 11, 25, 28 and 29 of the Women's Protection Act 2006 un-Islamic and unconstitutional on the premise that the overriding effect of the Hudood Ordinances over other laws could not be taken away, it also asserted that the jurisdiction to hear appeals under any law relating to ten offences covered by the term 'hudood' for the purpose of Article 203 DD of the constitution lies with the FSC and not the high courts."[170]

The penalty for a Zina offence (fornication, adultery) is harsh and can involve long prison sentence and corporal punishment. Under the Hadood Ordinance the maximum penalty is death.[171] There are reports of death sentences and executions in recent years. On 5 June 2007 one woman and three men were executed after having been found guilty of adultery in Alamgudar village.[172] On 18 July 2010 a couple in Manjakot Village in Khyper-Pakhtunkhwa Province were sentenced to death for adultery.[173]

Offences in relation to the Hadood ordinances are dealt with by procedures that are different from ordinary criminal offences and instead of a magistrate issuing arrest warrants these matters have to be presented to a Sessions Court in the first instance. For this reason, as was pointed out above, a charge of *zina* is often accompanied by an ordinary criminal charge in order to facilitate the prosecution and arrest of the target.

3.3 The risks to women without a male partner

Women who have been abandoned by their partners or persecuted by their families face further cultural barriers to establish a decent life. It is difficult for an unmarried to establish a life for herself in Pakistan given that she has no extended family network. It is rare for people to live alone in Pakistan. Even men will usually live with their families until they marry. For women this is especially difficult, as it is not considered acceptable for a woman to be without the protection of a male family member. Although it is not illegal for women to live by themselves, it is extraordinarily difficult for a woman to persuade a landlord to rent out an apartment or house. There are constant pressures of cultural opposition and personal security faced by women outside a family network.[174]

A single/divorced woman living alone will be stigmatized and ostracised by society. Being unmarried is a matter of profound shame, and parents do not usually encourage their daughters to return home after divorce as they will be a social pariah. There is virtually no possibility for a divorced woman to remarry or acquire a male partner as virginity is seen as a fundamental condition for acceptability as a spouse.[175]

Unmarried women (and this includes divorced women) cannot easily function in Pakistani society without a family network. Venturing out into the city alone or travelling is extremely hazardous and they will be subject to harassment from male vendors, bus drivers etc. Obtaining employment also depends on the family network and it is assumed that the husband or father will arrange for a woman to be employed. Female labour participation in Pakistan is very low (about 24%) and mostly concentrated in agriculture where women are supporting the family business.[176]

A report from the UNHCR cites the comment of a professor from the University of Warwick that summarizes the problem of unmarried women living alone in Pakistan:

"Generally, it would be accurate to say that single women are rarely able to live on their own without a male member of the family in Pakistan. Reasons for this are numerous, but they primarily stem from custom and culture that requires a woman to have a male family member to be in a protective and supervisory role. Society also frowns upon women living on their own and would not help the reputation of the single woman. You may find one in a single woman who has the means and can live in a big city with helpers, etc. to assist and protect her. This of course is a minority and an exception rather than the rule".[177]

Although there are some shelters run for women by the state and by NGOs, this is not a permanent solution for a woman at risk of attack. First of all the shelters do not provide adequate protection from illegal attacks, as there have been reports of women being attacked if they only briefly went outside a shelter, or when they were brought from the shelter to the court, and serious abuse of women inside shelters.[178] Secondly the state shelters largely house women who have been put there by a court order. Facilities provided by NGOS and the state have very limited capacity and can only provide for a very small proportion of the need. Women are usually permitted to stay at most three months in a shelter, so a shelter, even if the a woman could get access to one, would be at best a very temporary solution.[179] However, reintegration into society is not possible due to position of single women.[180] Pakistan has no services for destitute persons, the state expects the family to take care of their own. If the family is not available to take care of her, then there is nowhere for an unmarried woman to go.[181]

Another risk faced by women cut off from her family network is that her children may be taken from her either by force or through a legal process. Thus, it was reported: "In Mst. Imtiaz Begum v Tariq Mehmood, the Lahore High Court allowed the mother to keep the child till it had attained the age to receive formal education. According to the court, this age would be determined according to the custom of the area of parent's residence. The court stated that to set the age at seven or nine is not a requirement of Islamic law. If the age at which a child starts its school is made the standard for termination of custody, a mother will be allowed to keep the child till the child becomes three and a half years old as that is the age at which a child starts going to school in most of the Pakistani cities."[182] Other courts have taken the view that the mother should have custody until the girls reach puberty. In any case, the father will at some point have an iron-clad claim to custody over the children. If the children are taken from the mother by force, the general attitude towards family matters and the role of fathers as heads of the family means that it would be very hard, if not impossible, for the mother to force the return of the children into her custody.

3.4 The risks to members of the LGBT community

The risks to members of the LGBT community pose a dilemma for the authorities considering asylum applications. There is in UK society and therefore in the UK government a general commitment to support the status and rights of the LGBT community and protect it against discrimination. Moreover, the risks to members of the LGBT community are well established in an Islamic Republic in which homosexuality is completely taboo in society and homosexual acts are serious criminal offences. However, the UK authorities still do their utmost to deny protection to LGBT persons. The first step is to question whether in fact the applicant is homosexual or transsexual etc. It is not clear what competency the authorities have to make such a judgement, and the arguments present by the authorities on known occasions have been very superficial. Nevertheless, it is very common that they simply refuse to accept assertions by applicants with respect to their sexuality. The second step is to somehow assert that the risks can be mitigated. This is where they come into serious conflict with the country evidence.

In Pakistan, sexual relations between men are strictly illegal. The most explicit prohibition is contained in Section 377 of the Penal

Code: "Whoever voluntarily has carnal intercourse against the order of nature with any man, woman or animal, shall be punished with imprisonment for life, or with imprisonment of either description for a term which shall not be less than two years nor more than ten years, and shall also be liable to fine ....'"[183] This is also known as the law against "unnatural acts".

There is no provision in Pakistani law that protects the rights of gay persons. There is no protection against discrimination based on sexual orientation. Same sex unions are not permitted and persons who are openly homosexual or gay couples cannot adopt children.[184]

Although informal persecution of those suspected to be or having out as homosexual is more common than criminal prosecution, it nevertheless does occur, and men have been prosecuted for sodomy between men and men and boys. In 2010 there was a report about two men being prosecuted under Section 337 of the penal code and sentenced to 2 years in prison.[185] Offences under the Section 377 were recorded by the Peshawar High Court in 2012 and 2013.[186] Thus the IRBC reported about ten cases in Punjab prosecuted under Section 377 of the Pakistan Prosecution Code in 2011 in relation to gay men, of which two resulted in ten year prison sentences.[187]

Homosexuality is considered to be a grave violation of Islamic laws and from a cultural and religious perspective an abomination punishable by death. As the Norwegian Country of Origin Information Centre Landinfo reported: "There is no room for exposure of a gay identity in Pakistan... homosexuality represents a permanent threat to marriage and reduces a family group's opportunity for consolidation through marriage. Homosexuality carries a sense of and is in itself a source of the destruction of the patriarchal extended family. Homosexuality violates the Pakistani community's most important institution and it would probably be perceived as far more serious to come out with a homosexual identity than if homosexual acts were to come into public awareness.[188]

Violence against gay persons in the major cities of Pakistan such as Islamabad, Lahore and Karachi is common. Sometimes gay persons are abducted by persons pretending to be gay and subject to gang attacks which can include rape. Persons believed to be gay can also be subject to homicidal attacks by strangers.[189]

The paper "The News" reported the "lynching" of a gay by a mob: "The man was identified as Muhammad Hashim Jokhio, son of Meran. Jokhio was a watchman by profession and had been married for over 25 years but had no children. The murder took place in the limits of Shah Latif police station. According to eyewitnesses and some police officials, Jokhio was ostracised by fellow villagers for his alleged sexual preferences, and thus, he lived separately. "Late Friday night, a group of charged people raided his house, and allegedly found him 'getting intimate' with another man. The villagers then pounded him with clubs and rods, and killed him," they said. Shah Latif police were reluctant to reveal details of the events that led to the killing of the man but confirmed that the deceased was a 'homosexual'.[190]

In April 2014 a serial killer was arrested. He was accused of killing three gay men in Lahore because of their sexual orientation. Some news outlets in Pakistan described the killer as "the epitome of righteousness" by news outlets in Pakistan.[191]

The Immigration and Review Board of Canada reported: "According to Al Arabiya News, an English-language news service based in Dubai, most hate crimes against LGBT people in Pakistan are unreported or are out of the public spotlight (24 Aug. 2014). Similarly, the WEWA representative indicated that in cases in which gay men or lesbians are murdered, the family often does not report the motive of the crime in order to not dishonour the family, or claims it was an "honour killing" or a suicide (31 Dec. 2014)."[192] (WEWA refers to the Women Employees Welfare Association). As has been explained in the previous sections, the Hudood ordinances that define the offense of "zina" are relevant here. An offense of unlawful sexual intercourse (Zina) takes place wherever "a man and a woman ... wilfully have sexual intercourse without being validly married to each other" (Section 4 of the Zina ordinance).[193] But this can also apply to homosexual activities since any sexual relations outside a marriage relationship are deemed unlawful.

According to Dr. Matthew Nelson as regards the law against "zina": 'This law does not specifically target LGBT groups. However, insofar as non-heterosexual relationships cannot be legalised in any form of marriage, it suggests that non-heterosexual sexual acts that involve penetration can be prosecuted ... '[T]he legal punishment for zina (Sections 5 and 17 of the Ordinance) perpetrated by a Muslim is death. (For non-Muslims the punishment is lashing.)"[194]

Although cases against members of the LGBT community are not frequently brought, the very existence of the legislation can be considered a form of persecution as it forces LGBT persons to keep their sexual identity secret and conceal much of their life from the general public as well as frequently their families. Moreover, they can fall victim either to zealots who seek out opportunities to target homosexuals, or anyone in the personal circle who has a dispute with them or a grudge, or hates LGBT persons, and can bring a case against them that will literally destroy their life.

Members of the LGBT community cannot seek protection from the police, and this conforms to the perception of the general public in Pakistan of the police and the reality of the experiences that ordinary people have. Homosexual men in Pakistan cannot be open about their sexual orientation in their place of work. Those whose sexual orientation becomes known will face problems at work, harassment and are likely to lose their job. These attitudes were captured by the research of the Neengar Society. They conducted a workshop in which they found that even those participants who claimed to be open to having LGTB friends, 43 out of 45 participants stated they would not work with an LGBT person in their office. Moreover, openly homosexual persons not only run the risk of not finding employment or losing their jobs after revealing their sexuality, but they are open to criminal persecution as well.[195]

In the larger cities such as Karachi, Lahore and Islamabad it is impossible for homosexuals whose sexual orientation is known to rent an apartment or find any accommodation. It is actually very hard for single men and almost impossible for single women to rent an apartment by themselves, but openly gay persons will be denied accommodation. The police in Lahore has advised landlords to carry out proper checks of prospective tenants due to the conservative local culture. LGBT persons are largely confined to the worst areas of slums and at constant risk of losing their accommodation. In smaller towns and villages, the presence of openly gay persons would not be tolerated.[196]

In Pakistan gays have to live discreetly, but even if they do that does not mean there is no threat. In the culture of Pakistani society, it is not usually accepted that men, especially as they mature, remain unmarried, live alone or with another man. For this reason, most gay people get married and live with a woman.[197] This is what "living discreetly" means for gay persons in Pakistan. As for displaying public affection, that would get a gay couple in Pakistan attract brutal physical attacks immediately. It is also the case that the only way in which members of the LGBT community can exercise their human rights to live according to their sexual orientation is to break the law and commit serious crimes which are not offences under UK law. This is the case whether they are prosecuted for these crimes or not. Essentially, to return them to Pakistan is to make them criminals in that country.

CHAPTER 4

The blasphemy law and religious persecution in Pakistan

4.1 Christians in Pakistan

Pakistan is an Islamic Republic, which means that Islam is the state religion and Sharia law is practiced. Christians are a significant religious minority community in Pakistan, constituting about 1.6% of the population (2,800,000 people). Approximately half are Roman Catholic and half Protestants, but there are also some newer and older denominations. Although there is officially some religious tolerance and the constitution declares all people equal before the law, since the time of President Zia-ul-Haq there has been an increasing Islamization of the state and marginalisation of Christians as well as overt discrimination. Christians in Pakistan lack equal political, socio- economic status, they are barred from taking on leading roles in governmental institutions.[198]

Thus constitutionally, no Christian may become President, Prime Minister, Chairman of the Senate, or the Speaker of National Assembly (Parliament) of Pakistan. Under the Constitution, the policies and practices have been adopted by all government and judicial functionaries not to accept Christians at any level of government, so that almost no Christians are included in leading positions. None of the Christians are in a position as the Chief of Army, Navy, Air Forces, Paramilitary forces, police, etc. There are no Christian Commissioners, Deputy Commissioners, Assistant commissioners. In the judiciary, there are no Christian Judges in any High Court, while there are four High Courts, Supreme Court, Federal Shariah Court, nor is there any Christian judge working as a District Session Judge in Pakistan. The exact same situation prevails in Education and other departments.

Access to jobs and entries to get education at lower and higher levels have been closed under unwritten conventions. The Christian Educational institutions, which were running and managed by the churches were nationalized by the Bhutto government in 1972 and robbed of their Christian character. Due to the nationalization of Christian Educational Institutions and the abolition of the reserved seats for minorities in the government institutions in 1972, there has been an increase of the Christians in illiteracy and poverty. At present, 4% of the women and 8% of the men from the Christian community are literate. Therefore 96% women and 92% men are suffering of illiteracy and many of them live in poverty.

In recent years the threat to Christians both from extremists and the general population has intensified. Thus, Open Door USA has reported: "While long-standing historic churches have relative freedom in worship and religious activities, they are heavily monitored and regularly targeted for bomb attacks. Churches that are engaged in outreach and youth work face the worst of the persecution, although all Christians suffer from institutionalized discrimination. Occupations deemed as "dirty" and "shameful" are reserved for Christians, and many believers are victims of bonded labor. Pakistan's notorious blasphemy laws target religious minorities but affect Christians the most, especially those who seek to evangelize. Discussion of the Christian faith is also known to attract attention from radical Muslims, making it dangerous to engage in faith-related conversations."[199]

In a report in May 2016 the journal Foreign Policy published a report that concluded that fear was a daily reality in Pakistan. The report referred to the following incident: "In March 2015, in the weeks leading up to Easter, suicide bombers launched an assault on two churches in the Youhanabad neighborhood of Lahore, killing 19 people. Then on Easter Sunday this year, Lahore was struck again when another suicide bomber blew himself up near a selection of children's rides at the city's Gulshan-e-Iqbal park. At least 74 people were killed and hundreds more injured by the explosion. Among the slain were eight members of a single family. According to a spokesperson of Jamaat-ul-Ahrar, the Pakistani Taliban splinter group responsible for the attack, the primary target was Christians celebrating the end of Easter." [200] The article refutes however the often that there is "no general risk" to Christians in Pakistan or that the risk to Christians comes primarily from militants: "Yet what this analysis fails to take into account – particularly in the Christian context – is that the maltreatment of Christians in Pakistan is enhanced by militancy rather than driven by it. At an everyday level, the root causes of the anxieties of the community owe more to the actions of ordinary Pakistanis rather than terrorist outfits."[201] According to the renowned journal "Christianity Today", "Pakistan recorded the most violence against Christians last year. The country also scored the highest in church attacks, abductions, and forced marriages, according to Open Doors."[202]

The report emphasizes that animosity towards Christians is deeply rooted in Pakistan for social as well as religious reasons: ""In the case of Christians, both religion and class impact how they are treated in Pakistan and discriminated against," says researcher and writer Rabia Mehmood. "While religious intolerances are more widely highlighted there is also a deep-rooted, caste-based discrimination that has existed in South Asia for hundreds of years. For example, the derogatory term *"churha"* (sweepers) is commonly used to describe Christians. Historically most Christians in Pakistan are converts from lowly Hindu castes and the stigma and exclusion resulting from this has not left them."[203] The report also emphasizes that many Pakistani transfer their hostility to the United States to the Christian citizens as they perceive the United States as the leading political representative of Christianity in the world..

The Home Office Country Policy and Information Note, in the light of this report and other external evidence, seriously underestimates the risks to Christians in Pakistan. The fact that not all Christians are accused of blasphemy or killed does not take away from that. As the Foreign Policy Report states: "Taken together, these negative perceptions have created a combustible situation for the peace and security of Pakistan's Christian community. A measure of both their distress and how they are viewed by the mainstream Muslim population can be gauged from the horrific conditions with which Christians must contend on a day-to-day basis."

One particular threat to the Christian community is the forced conversion and marriage to Muslim men of Christian girls who are kidnapped. Complaints are routinely ignored by the police, and girls and women forced to marry a Muslim are pressured to say that the marriage was voluntary with the threat of the accusation of blasphemy and apostasy against them, which can provoke violent attacks or legal prosecutions against them. According to the Araut Foundation up to 700 girls are forced into marriage and conversion every year. The Christian community in Pakistan is embattled and has to contend with multiple threats on an everyday basis.

4.2 The Use of the Blasphemy Laws

Christians in Pakistan also face the potential of persecution by the state and by individuals. A particularly serious threat arises from the so-called "blasphemy laws" consist of several sections of Pakistan's Criminal Code § 295. § 295-A is a catch-all law that prohibits outraging religious feelings. § 295-B prohibits the defiling of the Quran. § 295-C forbids defaming the prophet Muhammad. Another provision in the law, contained in § 298 forbids the wounding of the religious feelings of another person, punishable by up to three years imprisonment and/or a fine. With the exception of § 295-C, an offence is only committed if it is the consequence of the intent of the accused. A conviction under § 295-B can result in life imprisonment, and a violation of § 295-C is punishable by death.[204]

Christians who follow the requirement of their religion to seek the conversion of others face the prospect of both legal and extra-legal persecution, including imprisonment, the death penalty or serious extra-legal violence. Although Pakistan does not have a law against apostasy as such, the blasphemy laws are used to bring charges against those who abandoned their Muslim religion using the provisions against outraging religious feelings and defaming the prophet Muhammad. Often such charges are brought by third parties who either have a grudge against the accused person or are outraged by their abandonment of the Muslim faith, believing that apostasy is an offence that needs to be punished by death. Those who are seen to be the cause of someone renouncing their Muslim faith are also dealt with ruthlessly.[205]

Courts in Pakistan have a record of convicting persons accused of such offenses on the flimsiest of evidence. Often the statements alleged to have been made by the accused are not precisely know since their repetition by an accuser would also constitute a like offense.[206]

The United States Commission on International religious Freedom reported in 2014 with respect to Pakistan: "The country's blasphemy laws ... target members of religious minority communities and dissenting Muslims and frequently result in imprisonment. Blasphemy laws are deeply problematic on a number of levels, and Pakistan's is especially so. The so-called crime carries the death penalty or life in prison, does not require proof of intent or evidence to be presented after allegations are made, and does not include penalties for false allegations. Further, the laws do not provide clear guidance on what constitutes a violation, empowering accusers to apply their personal religious interpretations. In September 2013, the Council of Islamic Ideology recommended against amending the blasphemy laws to add procedural safeguards, noting situations of misuse or fraud could be penalized through other sections of the Penal Code. In December, the Federal Shariat Court decreed that the death penalty is the only appropriate punishment for blasphemy."[207]

According to a report by Deutsche Welle in 2014 "On Tuesday, November 25, an anti-terror court in the semi-autonomous Gilgit-Baltistan region sentenced the owner of Pakistan's biggest private TV channel Mir Shakil-ur-Rahman to 26 years in prison for telecasting a "blasphemous" show. Veena Malik, a Pakistani actress and the host of the morning program, along with two guests on the show, were also convicted."[208]

Intellectuals with liberal ideas can easily come under threat. A particular example was the case of Junaid Hafeez, a lecturer at Bahauddin Zakariya University who was accused by hard-line student groups of making derogatory remarks against the Prophet Muhammad in March 2013. For a year no lawyer was willing to accept an appointment to defend the accused due to the risk of attacks from extremist religious groups. These fears turned out to be justified. Rashid Rehman, a human rights lawyer who took the case, was killed in his office in Multan by gunman for defending someone being prosecuted under the "blasphemy" laws.[209]

There are many examples of how Christians and others have fallen foul of the blasphemy laws for trivial actions or on the basis of accusations by people objecting to their Christianity or seeking to resolve disputes or acquire other people's property. For example, On 5 November 2014 a young Christian couple was beaten to death by a murderous mob in a small town of Kot Radha Kishan in Punjab province. They were accused of blasphemy and desecrating a copy of the Quran. The area is a political stronghold of former Prime Minister Nawaz Sharif. The likely cause was a dispute about work at the local kiln in which the bodies of the two Christians were subsequently burned.[210]

In June 2009, Asia Noreen, better known as Asia Bibi, a farm worker from the village of Ittan Wali in Sheikhupura District was asked to fetch water. When she brought the some of her Muslim fellow workers refused to drink the water as they considered Christians to be "unclean". Subsequently some co-workers alleged that Noreen had made derogatory comments about the prophet Muhammad and a mob came to her house, attacking her and her family before the police intervened. A police investigation into the matter resulted in her arrest and prosecution under the blasphemy laws (Section 295 C of the penal code). After spending more than a year in prison, she was sentenced to death by Judge Muhammed Naveed Iqbal at the court of Sheikhpura, Punjab. The case of Asia Bibi has attracted international attention, because the governor of Punjab, Salman Tasseer, supported her and called for a change in the blasphemy laws. Tasseer was murdered for his stand on the blasphemy laws.[211] In 2018 the Supreme Court of Pakistan overturned the conviction of Asia Bibi after she spent 8 years in prison. This judgement provoked nationwide protests in Pakistan on such a scale that the government was forced to put Asia Bibi on the exit control list to prevent her from leaving the country until the judgement could be reviewed.[212] It is worthwhile referencing the Asia Bibi case to show how interaction between Christians and Muslims can provoke calls for the killing of a person from large numbers of ordinary people in Pakistan.

The UK Home Office in its Country Policy and Information Note (September 2018) stated "...there are very strong grounds supported by cogent evidence to suggest the situation has deteriorated for Christian converts – in relation to accusations of apostasy resulting in blasphemy charges, and the extreme hostility faced by society and Islamists. (2.5.4) It seems however that the situation in the country may have changed even further since the most recent country guidance given the extraordinary anti-Christian passion stirred by the Asia Bibi case. The authorities have warned Christian communities in Pakistan about the increased risk: "The Pakistan police have sent a letter to all the leaders of Christian institutes warning them about possible terrorist attacks, organised in connection with the case of Asia Bibi. The alert issued by the Lahore Police Inspectorate states that terrorist organisations such as 'Tehrik-i-Taliban Pakistan' and 'Jamaat-ul-Ahrar' are planning attacks aimed at the Christian community, in reaction to Asia Bibi's acquittal, the Christian woman accused of blasphemy and acquitted by the Supreme Court on 31 October. The police urge Christian institutions to "pay attention to vigilance"..."[213]

In September 2009 Robert Fanish was found dead in his prison cell in Sialkot where he was held on blasphemy charges. The family, supported by NGOs, claimed he had been tortured by the police which caused his death. A report was drawn by an alliance of human rights groups, the Joint Action Committee for People's Rights.[214]

On 22 January 2009, a man called Hector Aleem was arrested for blasphemy. He was a Christian Human Rights Activist and Chairman of Peace Worldwide. The basis of the complaint contained in the FIR was that the leader of the Sunni Tehreek received a blasphemous text message from someone who once had contact with Aleem. As the actual perpetrator could not be found, Aleem was arrested and his house was raided by the police. Alleem was working for a church that was destroyed by the capital development authority in Islamabad on the grounds that it had been erected illegally, and he was threatened that if he continued to work for the church he and his sons would be killed and his daughters forcibly converted to Islam. He was tortured by the police after his arrest and eventually informed that he was being charged with blasphemy.[215]

In May 2008 Robin Sardar, a Christian doctor was jailed after he was accused of blasphemy by a Muslim street-vendor who wanted to install his business in front of his clinic.[216]

Walter Fazal Khan (84), a Christian, was accused by his servant Raja Riaz of burning the Quran in his house. Khan was arrested by the police under penal code 295-B. The accusation was, according to the family, part of a plan to take Khan's house and land from him. An allegation of burning the Quran against Naseem Ghani and Mohammed Shafiq in 2000 resulted in a sentence of seven years in prison.[217]

In March 2006, Shafeeq Lateef was arrested for making derogatory remarks about the prophet Muhammad and desecrating the Quran. In was sentenced to death on 18 June 2008 and fined 500,000 rupees.[218] The quality of police protection is variable throughout Pakistan, and the police is frequently complicit in the abuse of the blasphemy laws. Ordinary people in Pakistan do not expect the police authorities to protect them from violent attacks as was discussed in Chapter 2. Christians cannot expect protection from the authorities even against extra-judicial attacks. Indeed, almost all police officers are Muslims and would share the sentiments of the general population towards atheists, apostates and those guilty of blasphemy. However, the authorities are likely to persecute them themselves in the event that they are accused of blasphemy and such accusations are easily made and usually are prosecuted without any evidence.

There have been many reports of serious violence against Christians and others who are not Sunni Muslims for practicing their faith or for dissenting from Islam. Such violence is endemic and involves attacks against houses, property, the abduction of women for rape and the forceful conversion to Islam and marriage of abducted Christian girls and women and can also affect prominent persons in Pakistan. Those accused of blasphemy may be subject to harassment and attacks, as may those involved in such cases as lawyers, police and politicians.

On 2 March 2011 Clement Shahbaz Bhatti, a Pakistani politician and elected member of the <u>National Assembly</u> from 2008, and a Christian, was assassinated on his way to work in Islamabad. He was the first Federal Minister for Minorities] from 2008 until his assassination on 2 March 2011. Bhatti was an outspoken critic of Pakistan's blasphemy laws and the only Christian in the <u>Cabinet</u> and in the unique position of being a Christian in high office.

The terrorist movement Tehrik-i-Taliban Pakistan claimed responsibility for his killing, accusing him of blasphemy against the prophet Muhammed. Bhatti, a Roman Catholic, had received numerous death threats since he publicly spoke in support of Christians in Pakistan who were attacked in the Gojra riots 2009 in Punjab Province. He also supported Asia Bibi after she was sentenced to death for blasphemy in 2010, which further increased his profile and made him a special target and he suffered the same fate as the governor of Punjab, Salman Taseer.[219]

Examples of where people accused of religious offenses have been attacked or brutalised (rather than protected) by the police abound. In August 2003, a Christian called Samuel Masih was arrested by the police for allegedly defiling a mosque by spitting on its wall. In prison, Masih contracted tuberculosis and he was transferred to a hospital. On 24 May 2004, a police constable used a hammer to kill Masih in the hospital. He stated it was his duty as a Muslim to kill Masih. In 2008, Ashed Masih (38) Muslim extremists last Friday set him on fire for refusing to convert to Islam and raped his wife with the help of police. The incident occurred in front of a local police station. On 28 October 2007, the police arrested Muhammad Imran of Faisalabad under § 295-B for allegedly setting fire to a Quran. For three days, the police kept Imran in a torture-cell where they tortured him. Then the police sent him to a jail where other inmates attacked him. His jailers put Imran into solitary confinement without attending to his injuries. On 14 April 2009, an Additional Sessions judge released Imran. On 18 January 2011 it was reported that Pakistani police in Karachi had raped and murdered an 18-year-old Christian man and threw his body into the sewer. His father, Pervez Gill, faced threats from the police including death threats and threats to charge them him and other

Christians with religious crimes after filing a First Information Report against four policemen.[220]

On 13 April 2017 it was reported that a university student at Abdul Wali Khan University in Pakistan was tortured, beaten and killed by a mob who accused him of blasphemy. The student Mashal Khan was pursuing a course in journalism. He was apparently disliked by other students for his liberal and secular views. This very recent incident shows the dangers faced by anyone suspected of anti-Islamic views.[221]

The UK authorities have expressed the view with regard to the risk faced by Christians in Pakistan that Christians active in evangelism when someone who seeks to broadcast their faith to strangers so as to encourage them to convert, may find themselves facing a charge of blasphemy. This leads to the conclusion that evangelical Christians face a greater risk than those Christians who are not publicly active.

This effort to distinguish different levels of risks to different "types" of Christians reflects a lack of knowledge on the part of officials. The term "evangelical Christians" is normally used to referred to a particular fundamentalist orientation of Protestant Christians.[222] The accepted teaching in both Protestant denominations and the Catholic Church is that it is the duty of *every* Christian to evangelise.[223] The distinction made by Home Office officials between those who evangelise and those who do not, and the assertion that evangelism is associated with "public" activities has no basis in Christian teaching at all.

Once again: It is the duty of all Christians to proselytise. This is very central to Christian teachings. Such activities can be public or private, but in Pakistan even private activities of this kind also carry a very serious risk of a Christian being accused of blasphemy, as my examples demonstrate. What this means is that in order to avoid the risk of persecution, Christians in Pakistan often ignore one of the central precepts of their religion, which is to seek to convert others. Since it is illegal and can have very serious consequences to attempt to convert Muslims, Christians in Pakistan confine their proselytising efforts mostly to inspire "lapsed Christians" or other non-Muslims.[224] This is not how "evangelism" is understood in Christian teaching as practiced in the United Kingdom or elsewhere. Consequently,

Christians in Pakistan are forced by their social environment to alter their behaviour and this will apply without any doubt to the Christian asylum seekers if they are forced to return to Pakistan, whether or not they have participated in public proselytising activities.

It is important to note that the situation in Pakistan has changed since the most recent country guidance case. Political movements whose main objective is the enforcement of blasphemy laws have gained considerable political ground and politicians have a difficult time to restrain them. Whereas previously the attention of Pakistani activists against blasphemy focussed on the Ahmadi community, the Christians have now become one of their main targets. The acquittal of Asia Bibi by the Supreme Court in 2018 has acted as a political catalyst that has unleashed the anti-blasphemy and anti- Christian forces in the country. The situation has become dramatically more dangerous for all Christians.[225]

4.3 Threats to Christian communities and the possibility of protection from the authorities

Throughout Pakistan Christian communities are under threat. Moving to Christian villages or compounds cannot protect persons at risk as they are not safe from those who seeks to attack Christians or from the authorities seeking persons accused of blasphemy. It was reported that in 2013 an entire Christian village was burned down in the Lahore area. After police came to arrest Sawan Masih, a resident of Joseph colony, responding to allegations of blasphemy, a mob assembled and started to attack the colony and set fire to houses. The police watched while hundreds of buildings were burnt down. The individual concerned was detained, while the residents of the village had to flee as the entire colony was destroyed.[226]

There are reports of entire Christian villages being attacked by mobs. Thus, in May 2016 it was reported: "The small community of Christians in a remote village were forced to run for their lives after a crowd of more than 1000 people gathered outside their homes and demanded they convert to Islam. Campaigners say three quarters of the 300-strong population have now had to flee and are starving in the countryside without food or water."[227] A fatwa was issued against the young man at the centre of this incident, a businessman put a bounty on his head and it was demanded that he should be handed over and be burnt to death for blasphemy. The entire community in Chak was threatened.

"Today, fear and a sense of abandonment by the state resides in the collective consciousness of the Pakistani Christians." The report focussed on the bombings in Lahore's Gulsha-e-Iqbal targeting Christians: "The community and several rights activists think that the silence of Christians after last week's bombings in Lahore's Gulshan-e-Iqbal park is not only out of fear of militants. By the time I visited the neighbourhood in April 2015, more than 150 men and boys had been arbitrarily detained by the police for murder and vandalism." This relatively muted response is in contrast to the events in 2013, after twin bombings at the All Saints Church in Peshawar. This bombing resulted in the deaths of more than 80 people and provoked protests by young Christians in Lahore and Karachi. As the Al Jazeera reports states: "In addition to becoming victims of militancy, these protests were also consequences of years of abuse faced by the community through blasphemy cases and arson attacks by Muslim protesters on Christian settlements and villages. Like African and Hispanic Americans in the United States, Christians in Pakistan are victims of an unjust system and structural violence. Christians are not only "soft targets" for the militancy, but also victims of socioeconomic and political exclusion… Tough crackdowns on disempowered Christian people after the protests in the wake of attacks on their community have pushed Pakistani Christians up against the wall. This year, they barely brought out demonstrations after the suicide attacks." This shows that Christians now fear the authorities as much as they fear Islamic militants.[228]

The Al Jazeera reporter explains: "Back in Youhanabad I had met 60-year-old Javed Hidayat, a Christian mechanic. In the aftermath of the protests, the police had raided his home in the middle of the night and taken his son away without an arrest warrant. When I spoke with him, he told me that the police charged his son not just with murder, but terrorism. In his desperate attempt to reclaim his son, he lost hours and days of work to solely focus on his son's bail."[229] In short, Christians face a pervasive threat of persecution by violent extremists, the blasphemy laws, the authorities that are supposed to protect them in addition to the socio-economic exclusion and systematic discrimination with respect to access to jobs, accommodation and other services.

There is no possibility that Christians who suffer persecution could receive any credible protection either from the police or the military in Pakistan. Recent events demonstrate how quick police are to arrest persons accused of blasphemy. Thus 68 lawyers have been charged with blasphemy in May 2014 because they protested against the arrest of a colleague.[230] How seriously blasphemy accusations are taken is indicated by the fact that in January 2012 a cleric accused of blasphemy was sentenced to death by the Additional Sessions District Judge.[231] Relocation within the country will not mitigate the risks faced by refugees.

The case AK and SK (Christians: risk) Pakistan CG [2014] UKUT 00569 (IAC) confirmed that there is a problem about protection: "However, predominantly, the evidence suggests that there is a failure to protect Christians from attacks and the consequences of abusive allegations of blasphemy. Apart from the actions of the high courts in overturning unfair verdicts, no effective action is taken by the authorities to protect and defend Christians or to punish their attackers although it has to be said that the same applies to non-Christians accused of blasphemy. Whether this stems from an unwillingness or an inability to protect, is not the issue. Overall, there has been and there continues to be an insufficiency of state protection in cases where serious allegations of blasphemy are made and pursued, regardless of the religious faith of the accused. " (§226)

The notion that Christians under threat could approach the authorities to assist with any problems in relation to the threats he faces and rely on their protection flies in the face of what is known about the situation the police and other security organisations[232]. This was demonstrated by the case referred to above when on 7 May 2014 the lawyer defending a University lecturer accused of blasphemy was gunned down in Multan.[233] In line with the evidence cited in the previous sections it shows how the police is not able or willing to protect people against blasphemy accusations. Likewise internal relocation is not safe given that the police executing an arrest warrant or someone with connections with the security services could access the NADRA national database and locate any person, as was discussed in Chapter 2.[234] Every person who seeks employment, to engage in business or to rent or buy property needs to present an ID card with a NADRA identification code.[235] Anyone in the police or with connections to the police would also be able to access the NADRA system.

In the case AK and SK (Christians: risk) Pakistan CG [2014] UKUT 00569 (IAC) it is stated: "Relocation is normally a viable option unless an individual is accused of blasphemy which is being seriously pursued; in that situation there is, in general, no internal relocation alternative." (§247) This statement needs to be reconsidered. Although Pakistan is a country with a large population, the diversity of the population means that it is not so easy for a person to just disappear, relocate, and assimilate in a new community. Moreover, the NADRA system makes it very easy to trace a person's whereabouts, and can be accessed by anyone with sufficient determination and the proper connections do so.[236] This means that if a person is being targeted by non-state actors, there is a serious risk of persecution even in the event of relocation. Moreover, the recent public demonstrations against the acquittal of Asia Bibi have stirred up the population in a dramatic fashion and have substantially increased the risk to Christians in Pakistan, as has been acknowledged by the Pakistani authorities.[237]

Atheists face similar and perhaps even more serious risks. Although there is evidence that there are people in Pakistan who are atheists, the idea of being a Pakistani atheist is in itself problematic. Persons born into a Muslim family are assumed to be Muslims, and Islamic law considers the abandonment of the Muslim religion apostasy, a crime which is considered to be punishable by death. Those who were not born into a Muslim family are assumed to belong to some other religion and their religious identity is noted in their passport. There is no concept of not belonging to a religion. For this reason, atheists in Pakistan keep a very low profile and seek not to be publicly identified.[238] Atheists in Pakistan also face the potential of persecution by the state and by individuals, including prosecution under the blasphemy laws.

Atheists in Pakistan face the prospect of both legal and extra-judicial persecution, including imprisonment, the death penalty or serious extra-judicial violence. Although Pakistan does not have a law against apostasy as such (the effort in 2006 to pass such a law failed), the blasphemy laws are used to bring charges against those who abandoned their Muslim religion using the provisions against outraging religious feelings and defaming the prophet Muhammad.[239] Often such charges are brought by third parties who either have a grudge against the accused person or are outraged by their abandonment of the Muslim faith, believing that apostasy is an offence that needs to be punished by death. Those who are seen to be the cause of someone renouncing their Muslim faith are also dealt with ruthlessly.[240]

In 2017 a new campaign to combat blasphemy began with disappearances of prominent atheist activists and reports of their torture. On 22 March 2017 (~16:00) Abdul Waheed (aka Ayaz Nizama), a blogger and Vice-President of the AAAP was detained by Pakistan security services Rana Norman, another secular blogger was also arrested. The media reports stated that the two were arrested for uploading offensive content on social media and it was claimed that they received financial and technical assistance from the United Kingdom, the United States, Canada and the Netherlands.[241]

Thus it was reported : "Since the beginning of the year, government officials and the courts have agitated against supposed "blasphemous" content, claiming that dozens of people are under investigation, and that there is a need to remove masses of "blasphemous" content from social media in particular. On 27 February, the Islamabad High Court (IHC) directed the Pakistan Telecommunication Authority (PTA) to block pages or websites containing blasphemous material on social media. On 7 March 2017 the IHC summoned Interior Minister Chaudhry Nisar Ali Khan for the following day, on a contempt of court petition. The petitioner (Salman Shahid, through his counsel Tariq Asad) contended that the authorities including the PTA have failed to comply with a prior court order to block websites and social media accounts containing "blasphemous" material. The judge Shaukat Aziz Siddiqui issued said: "This matter requires immediate attention, otherwise, the patience of the followers of Holy Prophet (PBH) may run out of control."[242] As a result there has been an increase in the censorship of media and social media to suppress the opinion of liberals, secularists and agnostics/atheists.

The Interior Minister of Pakistan convened a meeting of the Organisation of Islamic Conference on "blasphemy" online with the purpose to position Pakistan as a leader in combating what is called "blasphemy". A prominent Member of the National Assembly, Pakistan Tehreek-e-Insaf (PTI) lawmaker Ali Muhammad Khan stated that those who believed that Pakistan should become a secular state should mend their ways or leave the country, an usual outburst for member of a political party in Pakistan founded in 1996 by former national cricket captain Imran Khan and perceived as centrist and opposed to corruption.[243] There is no doubt that in Pakistan there is now a much less liberal atmosphere in relation to free speech if it is considered to be critical of Islam, significant political pressure to enforce the laws against blasphemy strictly and therefore the risks for atheists/agnostics has increased substantially since the issue of relevant country guidance information by the Home Office.[244]

Atheists in Pakistan can at any time face very serious threats to their life as a result of their faith from the authorities or Muslim citizens of Pakistan.[245] Some insight into the life of atheists in Pakistan has been given by anonymous testimonies. One atheist person cited anonymously stated: " If some people found out who I really am, they'd kill me. Others would settle for feelings of resentment and hate... I am a man who hides in plain sight. I don't want to, but I must."[246] Another atheist who described life in an Islamic Republic as hell of an atheist or sceptic stated: "You cannot ask questions openly, you cannot refuse to believe in something that has been asserted without evidence. You cannot decide how you want to live because what you will think, and follow was decided even before you were born. The most likely scenario is that you will sell your life at the cost of your breath" "... growing up in Pakistan I learned that you have to learn Arabic, you have to be fluent at reciting the Quran, you have to honor all the holy months, you have to become a statue in honor of the Adhan ... You have to starve yourself during the whole month of Ramadan so that Muslims around you do not feel uncomfortable and you do not become the reason for them to break their fast unlawfully."[247] Unless atheists pretend to be Muslims, living a life they do not believe in, keep all their opinions to themselves, their life is at serious risk. There is the constant danger that if they somehow slip up, voice opinions that are unacceptable or they are forced into actions they cannot accept (forced marriage, various religious activities), they will be persecuted by individuals or accused of blasphemy. The threat to atheists does not only arises not just from the espousal of atheist philosophy, but the conversion from the Muslim faith.

4.4 The risk to non-Sunni Muslims in Pakistan

Religious intolerance is not confined to the rejection of other religions, but also to other forms of Islam that differ from the beliefs and practices of the Sunni majority in Pakistan. One particular example is the Ahmadiyya community in Pakistan. Another is the more substantial minority of Shia Muslims, Ahmadis are considered to be a heretical cult by other Sunni Muslims because they do not accept that Mohammad was the "final prophet". Under Pakistani Law enacted during the administration of President Zia, Ahmadis cannot claim that they are "Muslim". Ahmadis have fallen foul of the blasphemy laws for trivial actions or on the basis of accusations by people objecting to their faith or seeking to resolve disputes or acquire other people's property. There have been more than 300 cases where Ahmadis have been charged with blasphemy and the extremists are advocating violence and the use of the blasphemy laws against them.

Khatam-e-Nabuwwat against the Ahmadiyya Association in the United Kingdom. Earlier in 2010 there was an attack against Ahmadi mosques by gunmen in Lahore in which 93 persons, including some Britons, were killed. The Ahmadis claimed that the campaign of hatred was also directed against their people in the UK. Darshna Soni from Channel 4 reported: "Since the attacks in Pakistan, we've found worrying evidence that a campaign of hatred is spreading in the UK. We've spoken to Ahmadis who have been physically attacked in the street - and to others who've been sacked from their jobs because they've refused to convert."[248]

Lord Avebury, a human rights campaigner and Liberal Democrat peer, became involved in countering what he considered a hate campaign against Ahmadis in the UK. The Channel 4 investigation quoted him: "This is how it all begins. Shops boycotted, posters going up in windows, people sacked from their jobs."[249] The hate campaign against the Ahmadis has spilt over into other countries, especially the United Kingdom, but in Britain Ahmadis can count on protection from the authorities, whereas in Pakistan the authorities themselves will persecute Ahmadis.

The Independent Newspaper reported in October 2010 that Islamic satellite channels, "have played an instrumental role in recent anti-Ahmadiyya campaigning. This week Ofcom criticised the Ummah Channel for a string of three programmes broadcast shortly before and after the Lahore massacre in which clerics and callers alike said Ahmadis should be killed." In a programme with the title "Seal of the Prophethood" a cleric declared on this channel that is viewed in the United Kingdom: "Until now, whenever one has claimed to be a prophet the Muslim nation has issued fatwa that he should be killed. It is only that at present Muslims are weak and they do not have the power to slice such a man in two parts." The Ummah Channel which accessible through Sky broadcast a debate on 21 May 2010 on the status of Ahmadis within Islam. The Independent reported:" When a caller named Asim asked for a scholar to explain whether Ahmadis were legitimate Muslims the imam replied: 'Since the time of the Holy Prophet (peace be upon him) the Sahiba [knowledgeable scholars] have confirmed that anyone who believes in a prophet after the Holy Prophet is a kafir [unbeliever], murtad [apostate] and Wajib-ul Qatal [liable for death].' He later added: 'Until now, whoever has claimed prophethood, the Muslim Ummah has issued the fatwa for them to be killed. And all these false prophets have always been killed. It is only now that Muslims have become weak and they do not have the strength that they should cut such people into two.'" Subsequently Ofcom ruled that the Ummah Channel has breached broadcasting regulations in this broadcast. There is no doubt that extremists were publicly calling for violence against Ahmadis in the United Kingdom.[250]

The Independent reported specifically with regard to Khatam-e-Nabuwwat's statements on this: "'If the anti-Qadiani laws or the blasphemy laws are touched by anyone in Pakistan,' Imam Bawa said, 'then the 1953 Lahore agitation against the Qadianis will be repeated in the streets once more. The streets and roads of Lahore were filled with blood in that agitation.."

In July 2009 the Punjab Police arrested 32 Ahmadis of Lathianwala under PPC 295-C and other sections related to offences based on religion. The blasphemy charge was taken off after four months, but the Home Secretary of Punjab government wrote a letter to re-instate it.[251]

In 2011 Rana Sajeel Ahmad, a, Ahmadi school boy was charged with blasphemy with FIR no. 352 dated 15 December, 2011 in Police Station Khushab. He went into hiding in fear of his life. His father was also arrested under the Ahmadi-specific law, PPC 298-C.[252]

It is clear that once Ahmadis come to the attention of any "orthodox" Sunni Muslim leaders and they take offence at any statements or religious activities, they could issue fatwas or involve the authorities in persecuting them by invoking the blasphemy laws. Experience shows that it is practically impossible for the targets to defend themselves, whether the alleged offence occurred or not. So, whether or not the submitted documents are accepted, given their religious activities the risk is real.

In Pakistan persons who convert from Sunni to Shia Islam can face extraordinary risks in Pakistan as this is considered to be by many Sunnis as an abandonment of the true faith. This risk is exacerbated the increasing extremism and violence in Pakistan that has affected all strata of society as the growth of the terrorist organisations has led to increasing challenges of the social order in the country. One manifestation are the frequent attacks on members of Shia community by Sunni extremists. The various Sunni jihadist groups in Pakistan are deliberately attacking and killing Shia. Persecution of Shia is not necessarily confined to terrorists, because there is violence against "unbelievers" throughout their country.

There is no question that Shia Muslims and other minority sects in Pakistan are under a grave threat. This threat goes back to the very foundation of the Pakistani state after the partition of

India but became more serious after Zia ul Haq seized the Pakistani government in a coup in 1977. His key objective was to shape Pakistan into a Sunni Islamist state. This meant that there was not room for other forms of Islam. Most Sunnis consider their adherents to be non-believers.

The increasing extremism and violence in Pakistan that has affected all strata of society as the growth of the terrorist organisations has led to increasing challenges of the social order in the country. One manifestation are the frequent attacks on members of Shia community. The various Sunni jihadist groups in Pakistan are deliberately attacking and killing Shia.

The Iranian revolution resulting in a government dominated by Shia clerics and the Iran-Iraq spilled over into Pakistan's emerging sectarian conflict. Sunni militant groups began attacking Shia in Pakistan and Iraq provided funding for anti-Shia militant organizations. The Arab Gulf states also contributed to efforts to marginalize Pakistan's Shia, making Pakistan into a space for a sectarian proxy war between Sunnis and the Iranian supporters of the Shia.

The Afghanistan War against the Soviet occupation involved the Interservice Intelligence Services (ISI) in Pakistan in supporting the Taliban and other Islamic militants to fight the Soviet Union. But this gave rise to new campaigns of violence against Shia in Pakistan that have continued to this day. Although officially disapproved of by the Pakistani government, successive Pakistani governments have proved unable to resist demands for further restrictions and persecution of minorities through the blasphemy law and other measures. The security services are dominated by Sunnis many of which are sympathetic to militants who oppose and attack Shia Muslims.

Pakistan's sectarian killings by jihadi groups became more frequent when Hakimullah Mehsud was a top commander of the TTP. The TTP began targeting any sect of Islam that these Deobandi militants (a particular sect of Islam associated with militants) deemed to be "munafaqeen" (those who spread discord). In particular Pakistan's Shia came under attack (as well as Ahmedi and Pakistan's other religious minorities), so were Pakistan's massive Sufi population, frequently referred to as Barelvis. The TTP began openly attacking Sufi shrines as well as attacks on Shia.[253]

The threat to Shia Muslims in Pakistan and the inability of the state to protect those targeted was elaborated in a Pakistani newspaper report: " Incidents that have occurred throughout the years, that are a threat to freedom of religious practice and the various levels of institutional discrimination are as follows: Organizations whose mandate is to kill Shia and other religious minorities such as Tahreek-e-Taliban (TTP), Sipah –e-Sahaba (SSP)/ Ahle Sunnat Wal Jamaat (ASWJ), Lashkar-e-Jhangvi (LEJ), Jundullah, Jaish-e-Islam and other extremist splinter groups falling in the legal system. In the last 20 years, as many as 72 judges and prosecution lawyers requested to shift to another case, went on leave or refused to hear the case on personal grounds against the LeJ chief Malik Ishaq, his sons, deputy chief Ghulam Rasool and his sons. Malik was released by court on July 29, 2015 in 70 cases of killing, in which over 100 was killed. There is inability of the police and security forces to effectively protect the Shia, even when death threats are being received. This is despite intelligence provided on Shia and their locations to conduct target killings.[254]

As the "Let us Build Pakistan" movement has noted in its report on a database of attacks on Shia Muslims in Pakistan: "Since late 1980s, Shias belonging to all walks of life and all ethnic backgrounds have been targeted and killed in every possible way, at every possible place and area in Pakistan. In almost all incidents, Shias (as well as Sunni Sufis/Barelvis, Ahmadis, Christians etc) have been killed by Deobandi militants of the Sipahe-Sahaba Pakistan (SSP aka ASWJ aka LeJ) and Taliban. It may be noted that ASWJ-SSP (also known as Lashkar-e-Jhangvi LeJ) is the urban face of Taliban."[255]

The Sunni militant group Lakshar-e-Jhangvi (LeJ), a group affiliated with the Pakistani Taliban, views Shia Muslims as heretics and considers the killing of Shia to be religiously justified. They have been responsible for various attacks and massacres of Shia, including an attack on pilgrims in the bordertown of Taftan on 9 June 2014. The attackers went from one hotel room to another, killing pilgrims indiscriminately.[256] Their beliefs, however, are widely shared among Sunnis. Generally, Sunnis believe that Shia are not true Muslims and those who convert from Sunni Islam to Shia Islam are considered by many ordinary people as well as extremists to be apostates and the penalty for apostasy is death.

In 2013 it is estimated that 700 Shia have been killed in violent attacks and a similar number in 2014. According to the independent Human Rights Commission of Pakistan, an estimated 300,000 people have fled Baluchistan to escape persecution by militant groups. Most of the refugees belong to the Shia Hazara and Hindu communities and were at risk of sectarian attacks from Sunni militants. The situation has reached a stage where now expert talk about a Shia genocide in progress in Pakistan.[257]

For example, there have been reports of serious violence against Shia in Gujrat. In September 2013 it was reported that seven minority Shia Muslims, including a prominent community leader, shot dead by four unidentified men in Gujrat (Punjab). According to eyewitnesses, four armed men on two motorcycles reached the house of Shia leader Syed Fazeelat Shah at Jasoki village in Gujrat district of Punjab. The victim was sitting with his family members and friends when the assailants opened fire on them. The killed him, his son, son-in-law, two grandsons and two of his friends.[258] In November 2013 a senior director at Pakistan's Gujrat University (a prominent Shia Muslim) and his driver in the central province of Punjab were killed. Syed Shabbir Hussain Shah, director of student affairs at Gujrat University, was killed by gunmen on a motorbike spraying bullets at the car.

Shia Muslims are at serious risk in Pakistan. For example, Parachinar in the FATA, with majority Shia population, has seen the emergence of radical Saudi-sponsored Salafist groups, and sectarian violence has become a disturbing phenomenon, fueled by local and global terrorist organizations like the Taliban and ISIS. These terrorist outfits have committed horrendous crimes in this mountainous region, killing Shias and rendering them homeless. Situated along the line dividing Pakistan and Afghanistan, Parachinar is a volatile region where security situation remains fragile and people live dangerously. After the ouster of the Taliban from Afghanistan in 2001, many Taliban militants crossed over into this region and established sanctuaries there. They would often launch targeted attacks against Shias, forcing many of them to abandon their homes. Government forces, instead of helping unarmed people against armed militants, stood paralyzed."[259]

For example, in 2015 extremists targeted a Shia mosque in the city of Peshawar.[260] Peshawar is a stronghold of Sunni militants and a dangerous city. In a suicide bombing 19 people were killed. In 2017 there was deadly attack in Eidgah Market in Shia majority Parachinar city of Kurram Agency. Shia Muslims had gathered to buy and sell fruits and vegetables in the agency's major town. In a powerful explosion 25 persons were killed and over 60 injured.[261] In June 2017 twin terror attacks killed at least 75 people and injured over 300 there on Friday twin terror attacks killed at 75 people and injured over 300, again in Parachinar city of Kurram agency.[262] Attacks have also been reported in 2018.[263]

Serious attacks against Shia have been reported from all parts of Pakistan, including Karachi and the capital area of Islamabad and Rawalpindi. For example: " A suicide bomber in the city of Rawalpindi hurled a grenade into the midst of a Shia procession before detonating his vest and killing 23 people, while other attacks throughout the country from Karachi to Dera Ismail Khan claimed the lives of dozens more."[264] On 24 January 2017 Mohammed Kazim Raza (39), a Shia Muslim, was gunned down in a sectarian attack in Gulistan-i-Jauhar area of Karachi, in the night. On 22 February 2017 three persons who belonged to the local Shia community were shot to death under the Paroa Police Station area in Dera Ismail Khan District of Khyber Pakhtunkhwa. On 22 March 2018 it was reported that A Shia man was shot dead. Two others - including an infant - were injured in a vicious sectarian attack in Sachal area of Malir Town in Karachi.[265] An analysis published in "The Nation" laid out the failure of the state in Pakistan to provide protection to the Shia community: "The challenges faced by Shia are systemic and organised to debilitate and annihilate the Shia from practicing their religion without fear for their life or that of their loved ones. This systemic oppression takes several forms, whether it is the inability of Pakistan's judicial system or security apparatus to protect or bring to justice the criminals or the organizations carrying out genocidal killings, or the education system that has removed references to Shia school of thought, or media that refuse to cover the atrocities committed towards Shia, or spin the

genocidal killings as sectarian or as non-religious accidental killings…
There is inability of the police and security forces to effectively protect
the Shia, even when death threats are being received. This is despite
intelligence provided on Shia and their locations to conduct target
killings."[266] A report commissioned by Lord Avebury, Vice Chair
of the Parliamentary Human Rights Group, likewise used the word
"genocide" to describe the systematic persecution of Shia in Pakistan
and the failure of the state authorities to provide protection to the
victims or those at risk.[267] The Pakistani government has responded
to violence against Shia with at best indifference the fact is that there
very little has been done to respond to these attacks and there is clearly
complicity by security forces with the extremists. There is no question
that many in the police or other security services have sympathy with
those who attack Shia or other minorities. It is notable how authorities
have failed to apprehend or prosecute members of militant groups that
have claimed responsibility sectarian attacks.[268]

CHAPTER 5

Safety and security and human rights in Pakistan

Pakistan is a large country in South Asia that plays an important role in the geopolitics in the region. It is a nuclear power and a significant military power. Although ostensibly and Islamic Republic, it is in fact a secular democracy. But there are serious problems as the country is passing through an extremely dangerous period of instability. The conflict in Afghanistan, the activities of militant extremists from Al Qaeda and ISIS and the goal of militant extremists to bring down the Pakistani state and replace it with a sharia based kalifate have threatened the countries stability. The powerful position of the military which is more focussed on conflict with India rather than solving the serious security problems inside the country has compromised the role of civilian government and damaged civilian institutions. At the same time there are aspects of Pakistani culture, the importance of land and family, the concept of family and the prevalence of arranged marriages within the larger families, and the persecution of all who are not Sunni Muslims through the instruments of the blasphemy law that create serious risks for individuals and minority populations. This means that the country continues to experience a high level of political and social violence and the human rights of many people are compromised and not defended by the authorities.

PART II

Iraq

CHAPTER 6

Central Iraq

6.1 Introduction

The US-led intervention in Iraq in 2003 which resulted in the fall of the Baath Party regime led by Saddam Hussein transformed Iraq into an area characterised by enormous violence. This violence went through several different phases. The first phase was the intervention itself, the overthrow of the Baath Party regime which was accompanied by considerable resistance even though the Iraqi Army itself collapsed fairly quickly. The second phase was characterised by an insurgency which focussed around the Sunni tribes especially in the Anbar governorate and escalated considerably as a result of the founding and actions of Al Qaeda in Iraq led by Abu Musab al-Zarqawi. The presence of US forces provided a target-rich environment for Al Qaeda which had lost much of its capacity by the intervention in Afghanistan after 9-11. The surge of US troops accompanied by a new counterinsurgency strategy led by General David Petraeus as well as the cruelty of Al Qaeda in Iraq convinced Sunni tribal leaders to work with the Americans, resulting in considerable reduction in violence due to the insurgencies. But after the Obama administration pulled out all US troops from Iraq, the Islamic State of Iraq and the Levant (also known as ISIS and by its Arab acronym Daesh) which ISIL was founded as *Jama'at al-Tawhid wal-Jihad* in 1999, initally pledged allegiance to <u>al-Qaeda</u> and participated in the <u>Iraqi insurgency</u>

following the <u>2003 invasion of Iraq</u> as Al Qaeda In Iraq received an new lease of life as part of the anti-government insurgencies in Syria under the leadership of Abu Bar al-Baghdadi who declared a caliphate in 2014. ISIS/Daesh established an "Islamic state" in Syria and Iraq, with the Syrian city of Raqqa as its capital. It occupied considerable territory in Syria and Northern Iraq, eventually occupying the city of Rama in Anbar province. ISIS/Daesh consolidated its rule in occupied territories with extreme violence and against security personnel as well as civilians, executing a very large number of people on the flimsiest of grounds (including by public crucifixion), massacred minority populations such as Shia, Yazidis and other and used captured women as sex slaves for its fighters. It attracted a significant number of foreign fighters, many from the United Kingdom and other European countries. The Obama administration redeployed over 5,000 troops to the region to fight ISIS, but its role was mostly to guide Iraqi and Kurdish troops. The United States also used airpower with over 10,000 sorties to attack ISIS in its strongholds. The Trump administration persisted with the same strategy, increasing the number of troops and using airpower even more intensively but without fundamentally changing the approach. The Iraqi Army together with a collection of some 40 militias with almost exclusively Shia fighters under the umbrella of the PMU (Popular Mobilisation Forces - *al-Hashd ash-Sha'abi*) conducted operations to dislodge ISIS/Daesh from its territories. The fighting was extremely violent due to the scorched earth strategy of ISIS/Daesh and the intensity of their resistance, resulting in large-scale casualties among the security forces, ISIS fighters and civilians, especially in the urban areas. ISIS/Daesh most lost of its territories by 2017, including the city of Mosul, and its last territories in March 2019.

The military defeat of ISIS/Daesh was seen by UK authorities as a complete change in the regional situation accompanied by a decline in violence and making it possible to send asylum applicants from the region back to Iraq. However, there were many reports that the PMU were engaged in massive violence and human rights violations, especially against local Sunni populations, so much so that many observers considers the PMU more violent than ISIS/Daesh itself.

Although ostensibly under the control of the Iraqi Army, they proved to be a law unto themselves.

The total number of people killed in Iraq since 2003 remains a matter of debate since hard figures cannot be obtained. The Chilcot Report that investigated the role of the UK government in the intervention in Iraq explicitly declined to provide any estimates of casualties. The Iraq Body Count put the total number of deaths at 240,000, but other studies have higher figures, estimating the total deaths (in addition to the deaths that would have naturally occurred) since 2003 at 450,000. Iraq remains a country characterised by extreme violence, with about 120,000 fighters in various militias who are engaged in all manner of criminal activities, extortions, kidnapping and punishment of political opponents. Although the authorities in various European countries accept that there are regions of Iraq where the level of violence is too high for persons to be returned there, they still seek to return all applicants to Iraq, if at all possible, and become increasingly inventive at constructing arguments to justify it. One of the key problems is that as there have been various phases of more intense violence that no one could predict, it is unclear how justified it is to use data on body counts over recent months, for example, to characterise the risks because again and again intense violence has flared up in a manner that nobody could foresee, the most latest being the conflict between the United States and Iran which caused the United States to evacuate non-essential personnel from Iraq.

6.2 The risks to Sunni in various parts of Iraq

The risks of persecution and human rights violations are particularly high for Sunnis after the Shia majority took over the reins of power and due to the influence of Iran and the large number of fighters in Shia militias. This does not mean that the general level of violence in Iraq does not pose personal risks to all Iraqis, including Shia civilians.

If we start considering the situation in central Iraq, Baghdad is a city where majority Arab Shia and Sunni live in addition to minority Kurds and Christians and where there is still a considerable risk of violence. Currently, many paramilitary Shia groups operate in

Baghdad without clear chain of command. Although these groups have strengthened the front against ISIS, they are accused of practicing violence against Sunnis and others. In fact, Shia Muslim militias have engaged in widespread killings and kidnappings of Sunnis under the guise of fighting against ISIS. According to Erin Evers, a research with Human Rights Watch: "While the world rightly watches Islamic State abuses with horror, these abuses do not justify equally horrific abuses by Shia militias, who are operating in tandem with the Iraqi government."[269]Among the Shia Militias are Asa'ibAhl al-Haqq, the Badr Brigades and Kita'ib Hezbollah who all claim their fight is against ISIS. However, these militias are kidnapping and killing innocent civilians all over Iraq and there are no authorities that restrain them. The Asa'ibAhl al-Haqq Iraqi is paramilitary group also known as the Khazali Network, with over 3,000 followers. It is known that this group is supported by Iran's Quds Forces. It is part of their modus operandi to threaten Sunni Muslims given that in Mosul all Sunnis are believed to be under the control of ISIS and Sunnis coming to Baghdad are viewed as possible agents of ISIS. The Badr Organization is an Iraqi political party, previously known as the Badr Corps or the Badr Brigades, a militant group that fought against the US-led coalition in the 2003 Iraq war. The militia is still active even though some of its fighters joined the Iraqi army. The Kita'ib Hezbollah or Hezbollah Battalions is another Shia Iraqi insurgent group receiving funds, training and logistics from Iran's Quds Force. These militias, even though the Iraqi authorities support them to fight ISIS, are not only terrorist groups, but they are also thoroughly criminalized. It is important to note that Sunnis are the main targets of these criminal gangs, they and are ready to kill anyone who thinks stands in their way or in the course of extortion or other criminal activities.

In fact, Iraq is experiencing severe sectarian conflict once again. The government-backed Shia militias kill, torture and hold for ransom any Sunni whom they detain. Although ISIS has committed gross atrocities and mass killings of Shia, Shia militiamen are engaged in a campaign of retaliation which means that Iraq is returning to the levels of sectarian violence reminiscent of the Sunni-Shia civil war of 2006-07. At that time tens of thousands were murdered. Likewise,

Sunni militants, including supporters or members of ISIS are targeting Shia Muslims in Baghdad and other parts of Iraq.

According to an Amnesty International Report, the Shia militias have become the main fighting force of the Iraqi government since the army was defeated by ISIS when it overran northern Iraq in June 2014. The report states that militias enjoy total immunity in committing war crimes against the Sunni community. In particular they often kidnap Sunnis and demand large ransoms but kill their victims even when the money is paid. The militias treat all Sunnis as ISIS supporters.[270] The authorities cannot provide protection as the militias are acting on their behalf, ostensibly to provide security. At the same time there are ISIS (Daesh) sleeper cells throughout the country. Thus, during a visit to Baghdad in January, 2018, Gavin Williamson, the UK Minster of Defence stated that the war on ISIS in Iraq is "far from over", and that the war against ISIS "enters a new phase".[271]

Donatella Rovera, Amnesty International's senior crisis response adviser has stated: "Shia militias are way more important than the army and are running the show."[272] The government would have serious difficulty in bringing them under control even if it wanted to and police and the armed forces are penetrated by militia agents. But rather than trying to control them, the militia gunmen often act in co-ordination with the police and army. They target Sunni, Christians and others outside the Shia community. Ordinary Sunnis generally consider it unwise to have any contact with the police, knowing that they could be detained and tortured without cause. This explains the initial support of Sunnis for ISIS (Daesh) as they were suffering severe oppression from the Shia led government.

Since 2003, sporadic car and suicide explosions by Sunni militants and unknown perpetrators are repeated in Baghdad.[273] In July 2014 ISIS claimed responsibility for a series of car bombings in mainly Shiite neighbourhoods of Baghdad that killed at least 27 people.[274]In June 2014, as Islamic extremists threatened Baghdad, residents of the Iraqi capital started to flee on foot, emptying grocery stores and hiding in shelters to escape the anticipated bloodshed. One Baghdad resident told foreign reporters that his local market was "deserted" as his neighbours were afraid of the militants, whose brutality was deemed to far exceed that of Al Qaeda.[275] ISIS (Daesh) are Sunnis and consider

Shiite Muslims to be "unbelievers," and Baghdad has a majority of Shiites. Although the threat to Baghdad from outside has now receded to some extent because of coalition air strikes and Iraqi army operations, ISIS fighters are still operating close to Baghdad and have operatives inside Baghdad that can launch attacks. The fact is that Shia Muslims in Baghdad are also at serious risk of sectarian violence. Another serious terrorist attack in Iraq occurred on 13 January, 2018 that targeted convoy of the head of Baghdad's provincial council. [276] On 2 May a terrorist attack in northern Baghdad resulted in seven casualties.[277] A week later there was a suicide bombing that killed eight persons in the same area.[278]

In addition, some areas surrounding Baghdad are unstable and contested.[279] The majority of Baghdad public areas are not secured.[280] Even the Shia city-district of Sadr is not secured although it has better level of security.[281] Only few areas are secured and heavily guarded like the green zone where the embassies and governmental offices are located.[282]

The situation in Iraq remains tense as ISIS (Daesh) continues to regroup to launch terrorist attacks. Currently, civilians are attacked by both Shia and Sunni groups in the majority Iraqi Arabic regions of the middle and south. However, civilians are facing severe conditions in the areas under the control of Daesh (ISIS) and the contested areas which are usually majority Sunni areas.[283]

The FCO states that "the security situation throughout Iraq remains uncertain and could deteriorate quickly… Terrorists are very likely to try to carry out attacks in Iraq. There's also a high kidnap threat."[284] Private risk analysis companies are advising any foreign business persons to leave Iraq immediately, including Baghdad, reflecting on the general state of security.[285]However, when Daesh (ISIS) took over large portions of the country it became very quickly evident that these forces were not combat ready and could not prevail against a force that only numbers at most 5% of the Iraqi armed forces. When ISIS forces entered Mosul in June 2014 two army divisions disintegrated as thousands of soldiers and police officers dropped their weapons and uniforms and fled.[286] In May 2015, the extraordinary weakness of the Iraqi security forces was demonstrated once again when the city of Ramadi fell to a relatively small number of Daesh fighters as the numerically superior Iraqi army withdrew.[287] Whatever their successes may be, the fact is that Iraqi authorities are unable to secure most of Baghdad and provide protection to their citizens. The militias are completely out of control. In fact, for civilians like the applicant, the authorities in Baghdad are a threat as they give free reign to the militias who wantonly attack civilians as part of their general campaign of violence ostensibly to fight ISIS. Since the country guidance case of AA there have been renewed high profile attacks by ISIS against civilians Baghdad. In one such wave of attacks more than 100 people were killed in one day.[288] Moreover, the invasion of the Green Zone (the high security zone where government buildings are located) by followers of the Shia militia leader Muqtada al-Sadr demonstrated that the government cannot even protect the most vital and secure areas in the city.[289] On 3 July 2016 there was a massive attack on shoppers in Baghdad at the end of the Ramadan period that killed 215 people, demonstrating the risks to civilians against indiscriminate attacks by Daesh (ISIS) in Baghdad.[290] In January 2018 two suicide bombers blew themselves up in a busy market in central Baghdad, in back-to-back explosions that killed at least 38 people. At least 105 people were injured in the explosions.[291] In May 2018 eight persons were killed and dozens injured as a result of suicide attack on a funeral in Baghdad.[292]

In consideration of the risks of returning Iraqi nationals to Iraq "UNHCR and Amnesty International who considered that states should not deny Iraqi nationals international protection on the basis of internal flight alternative."[293] Persons (and especially Sunni Muslims, and Kurds) who are not known in the city, have no family network to support them are often viewed with suspicion as possible agents or supporters of ISIS (Daesh) and have little experience in avoiding the dangers in a city where militias supplant the police or and government security forces are especially at risk. Access to housing or employment is much harder for Sunnis in Baghdad without a family support network and many internally displaced persons are reduced to a below poverty level subsistence in camps.[294] However, the security risks outlined in this report also affect persons with a family network and entire families can become the target of sectarian violence.

Following the September, 2017 Iraqi Kurdistan referendum crisis, Kurds who lived outside the Iraqi Kurdistan region in the central and southern regions of Iraq were targeted and threatened by Shia militants and politicians.[295] Some Iraqi Shia politicians warned Kurds who endorse the referendum of revenge. Sa'ad Al Moutalibi, a prominent member in the ruling Shiite State of Law Coalition stated in a televised interview: " If the Iraqi Kurdistan region moves forward to the independence, the Kurds of Baghdad will not be permitted to live in the capital".[296]

The level of killings in Baghdad city is still so high that Baghdad has been considered the top city of the world ranked by risks of terrorism.[297] The civilian casualty figures which have fluctuated considerably over the last ten years are disputed and there is evidence that the security services themselves or the criminal militias operating on their behalf perpetrate attacks against civilians that are not officially reported.[298] The cities' most secure places, such as luxury hotels, still are subject to deadly attacks. People die everywhere, public transport is not secure.[299] In January 2018, a suicide vest attack occurred against a checkpoint in Baghdad resulting in over 12 casualties. Two days later, two suicide attacks killed over 36 civilians in central Baghdad. The attacks were directed against Iraqi day laborers looking for work. ISIS (Deash) claimed responsibility. The United States government in its 2018 reported considers the risk of terrorist attacks in Bagdad to be at the highest level (critical).[300]

The level of killings on a monthly basis, the fact that security forces arrest persons and detain and torture them on a regular basis without cause, the continuing sectarian strife, the uncontrolled actions of militias who are more powerful than the police and the appearance of unsanctioned, illegal checkpoints where people are arbitrarily detained and executed, all of this is reflected in the reports from individuals that despite the appearance of normalcy in some parts of the city they do not feel secure.[301] Added to this is the fact that there are frequent indiscriminate killings using improvised explosive devices, that the belt around Baghdad is acknowledged to be very insecure and that the country is at war, with the enemy penetrating the capital city on numerous occasions. As the Norwegian Country of Origin Centre reported in 2015: "There seems to be no areas of Baghdad that may be considered as more exposed to conflict related violence than others. What we see is partly warfare, and partly acts of terrorism against civilians, both taking place in parallel. Both may occur across the city. However, warfare seems to dominate in the suburbs. Since violence strikes so broadly, no particular group may be considered to be out of risk of being struck by violence in one form or the other."[302] There is an issue in relation to the reliance on data relating to murder rates that are unreliable and most likely underestimate the number of killings. The assessment of security in Iraq also needs to take into account the sectarian aspect of the violence and the emerging tribal conflicts. More recently cities in Iraq including Baghdad have experienced severe social unrest and violence due to popular discontent with the lack of provision of basic goods and services.[303] Moreover, it is important to consider that the existing situation is unstable and can change at any time. For example, nobody predicted that ISIS (Daesh) would be able to occupy the city of Ramadi. Nobody predicted that the Iraq armed forces and the Shia Militia would suddenly drive out the Peshmerga out of Kurdish occupied disputed regions in northern Iraq in 2017 which meant that all previous country guidance in relation to those areas was no longer fully applicable. Once returned to Iraq, individuals are at the mercy of a changing security situation that they are powerless to affect.

In a society where there is such a high level of conflict and sectarianism, where local areas are defined by tribal identities, it is difficult for a person to relocate to another area where he/she has not family or tribal network. In Baghdad the applicant will effectively be an internally displaced person. The situation relating to IDPs in the Baghdad area has reached crisis proportions: "There are more than 3.3 million Iraqis displaced in their own country and Baghdad alone houses more than 600,000 displaced people. These are families who were living in their towns or villages and have now lost everything. Many live in unfinished buildings, in schools, mosques or in makeshift settlements, often in very difficult and poor conditions. In Abu Ghraib in particular, we see that people suffer from limited access to water, poor sanitation facilities and overcrowded housing. These conditions are exacerbated by the impending summer with temperatures reaching up to 50 degrees.[304]

The risk to Sunnis in Iraq is such that many Sunnis in Iraq feel at risk just because of their name and there are reports of persons being killed because of their name. For example, there was a report of an occasion when 16 people named Omar turned up dead in Medical City, Baghdad, all killed apparently because their first name that reference the second Caliph in the Sunni version of Islamic history.[305] Having a Sunni name can result in discrimination as well as persecution. The situation is even worse for Sunnis of Kurdish ethnicity.

Sunnis (and especially Kurds) can also be at high risk in the southern governorates of Iraq. Al Jazeera reported in 2014 how sectarian militias targeted Sunnis, kidnapping persons and putting crosses on the doors of Sunni households in Basra.[306] In 2013 it was reported that Shia militias were carrying out systematic ethnic cleansing against Sunnis in southern Iraq.[307] After the Camp Speicher massacre near Tikrit where ISIS (Daesh) massacred close to 1,700 Shia (Iraqi military recruits)[308], the Shia militias in other parts of Iraq have been taking revenge against Sunnis. Deliberate targeting of Sunnis by Shia militias throughout Iraq continues apace in 2016.[309] The US State Department reported widespread violence due to tribal feuds.[310]

In addition to the threat of violence Sunnis and especially Kurds face in many parts of Iraq, there is also systematic discrimination against them in employment, provision of services and how they are treated by the security forces. Such discrimination has given rise to demonstrations against the Iraqi government which is perceived as favouring Shia and failing to control Shia militia.[311]

CHAPTER 7

Northern Iraq and the Kurdish Region

7.1 The evolving security situation in Northern Iraq

The security situation in Iraq remains unsafe and highly dangerous as non-state agents of persecution still commit acts of violence with impunity, the levels of violence in the central Governorates of Baghdad, Diyala, Kirkuk, Nineveh and Salah Al-Din as well as other parts of Iraq remained very high, access and residency restrictions apply; relocated individuals face extraordinary hardships in ensuring even basic survival. The UNHCR stated that asylum seekers that originate from Kirkuk as well as other governorates mentioned above should not be returned and should benefit from international protection. Likewise Amnesty International has pointed out the severe risks for any Iraqis returned to the country and has called for the practice of some European countries to return refugees to Iraq to be ended.[312] These recommendations were issued prior to ISIS (or ISIS) taking control over significant territories in Iraq which has increased the danger to individuals substantially.

The liberation of Mosul and surrounding regions in 2017 has resulted in a dramatic change in the nature of conflict in Northern Iraq and the Kurdish region. The liberated areas have been occupied by the Iraqi army and the Popular Mobilisation Forces. For civilians, the areas from which ISIS (Daesh) have been expelled have not necessarily become more secure. Iraqi troops have committed atrocities themselves. The Popular Mobilisation Forces (referred to as PFM or Popular Mobilisation Units PMU) consist primarily of Shia militias. As Amnesty International reported: "Government forces, paramilitary militias and the armed group Islamic State (IS) committed war crimes, other violations of international humanitarian law and gross human rights abuses in the internal armed conflict. IS fighters carried out execution-style killings targeting opponents and civilians fleeing IS-held territory, raped and otherwise tortured captives, used civilians as human shields and used child soldiers. Militias extrajudicially executed, forcibly disappeared and tortured civilians fleeing conflict, and destroyed homes and other civilian property. Thousands remained detained without trial on suspicion of links to IS. Torture in detention remained rife. Courts sentenced terrorism suspects to death, frequently after unfair trials. Executions continued at a high rate."[313] Just like during the occupation by ISIS (Daesh), local people are summarily executed by being handcuffed and thrown from buildings, beaten and tortured in a new rule of terror.[314]

The UNHCR has highlighted the atrocities committed against Sunnis during and after the liberation of territories from ISIS (Daesh): "The UN and human rights organizations have documented extensive abuses committed by elements of the PMUs, and in some cases the ISF, against fleeing civilians, particularly Sunni Arab men and boys, who are broadly perceived as supporting ISIS, irrespective of the existence or absence of evidence linking an individual to ISIS. Reported abuses include arbitrary arrest, abduction, physical abuse, enforced disappearance, summary killing and mutilation of corpses, including, for example, during military operations to retake the town of Fallujah (Al-Anbar) and surrounding areas from ISIS in May/June 2016. Hundreds of men and boys reportedly remain missing after having been taken into custody by forces affiliated with the PMUs. The media also reported arson and looting after forces affiliated to the PMUs entered Fallujah. Despite public announcements by the Iraqi authorities on the accountability of those involved in abuses against civilians, it often remains unclear if investigations have been conducted or prosecutions initiated."[315]

On 25 September 2017 the Kurdish Regional Government (KRG) held a referendum on the independence of the Kurdish region including all the areas occupied by the Peshmerga during the referendum. About 93% of those who voted supported independence. The results of the referendum were immediately rejected by the Iraqi government who consider the referendum unconstitutional and the KRI as part of the state of Iraq and ordered the KRG to surrender control over its two international airports.[316] The Iraqi government also demanded closure of the land crossings into the KRI.

As a result of the referendum, even though the KRG leadership offered to suspend implementation of the result, the KRI and the rest of Iraq are now effectively in conflict. Iraqi troops reinforced by units of the Popular Mobilisation Forces entered various disputed territories held by the Peshmerga. They occupied the city of Kirkuk, most of the oil fields under the control of the KRG and the cities of Niniveh and Diyala.[317] On 16 October 2017 the Iraqi forces supported by the Shia militias of Public Mobilization Unites or Forces (PMU, PMF) started to take control of the disputed territories, which were under the control of Kurdish forces. These areas include:

1. Kirkuk province.
2. Tuz-Khurmatu, which is part of Salahaddin province.
3. Mosul province areas including Sinjar, Zumar (in the north of Mosul including Mosul Dam), and Rabia.
4. Erbil province area of Makhmur. Note: Although Makhmur is part of Erbil, it has been officially dealt with by the Iraqi central government as part of Mosul.
5. Khanaqin area, which part of Diyala province.

Since 16 October 2017 tens of thousands, mainly Kurds, fled the disputed areas. In its 21 October report the UN stated that over 100,000 civilians fled from Kirkuk, Makhmur and Tuz Khurmatu.[318] In addition, the PMF have perpetrated violations against human rights in the disputed territories. The UN stated that "the United Nations is concerned about reports regarding the destruction and looting of houses, businesses and political offices, and forced displacement of civilians, predominantly Kurds, from disputed areas".[319] This was also repeated in the UN report of 21 October, 2017, which stated that "we are extremely concerned by reports of violence, looting and destruction".[320] Amnesty International also reported crimes against humanity by PMF/PMU, mainly targeting Kurds in Tuz-Khormatu near Kirkuk.[321] Displacement out of disputed areas, especially from parts of Zummar and Rabia (Niniveh Governorate), continued due to clashes between the Kurdistan Regional Government (KRG) and Central Government. A number of recently returned families are coming back to camps from disputed areas due to widespread destruction of their homes and the lack of resources to rebuild.[322]

Northern Iraq remains a war zone, with the KRG Peshmerga, Iraqi Army and the PMF pursuing their own objectives that are in conflict with each other, and with the alarming growth in private militias that are under nobody's control. According to a recent report by the renowned international relations institute IRIS in France: "A number of PMF militias operate in Iraq and Syria, crossing the border to fight alongside Syrian government allies. Therefore, the border areas north and south of IS territory are highly strategic for the PMF to sustain contiguous territory between Iran and Syria and sustain a trade route, explaining PMF encirclement of Tel Afar as part of the need to clear trade routes of rebellious elements. This is putting the militias at odds with other actors including the Peshmerga, where armed clashes in disputed areas of Diyala, Kirkuk and Sinjar have led to casualties, and US backed Syria proxies the Kurdish Syrian Democratic Forces and rebel groups north of the Jordanian border near the Baghdad-Damascus highway. This will complicate efforts to retake Qaim, Rawa and Ana located in this area. Certain elements of other Iraqi forces under the Iraqi Security Forces umbrella are also perceived as being sectarian and of working alongside and taking orders from the more powerful PMF militias, like the Federal Police and ERD."[323] This explains the high level of insecurity affecting locals and especially Sunni Kurds. Young men with no family network, no accommodation, no source of income are at grave risk of being recruited into local militias ruin by tribal leaders or neighbourhood vigilantes.[324]

Amnesty International report accused PMU/PMF Shia militants of crimes against humanity including "enforced disappearance and abduction of thousands of mainly Sunni men and boys, torture and extrajudicial executions as well as wanton destruction of property".[325] Human Rights Watch also reported similar violations.[326]

Reports of the UN and human rights organization documents the fled of tens of thousands of civilian, mainly Kurds from the areas taken by the Iraqi militants towards the areas controlled by Kurdistan regional Government (KRG).[327] UN High Commission of Refugee (UNHCR) stated that "an estimated 165,7801 individuals (27,630 families) have been displaced after Iraqi forces began moving into the disputed areas on 16 October". [328]

Security conditions in the areas taken from the Kurdish forces by the Iraqi and Shia militants have deteriorated and ISIS (Daesh) conducted attacks in these areas against both civilians and militants.[329] A twin suicide attack by ISIS inside Kirkuk left 5 dead and about 20 wounded including Iraqi militants and civilians.[330] In an earlier attack, which was carried out by a group of ISIS (Daesh) militants against Iraqi forces and at least four Iraqi militants were killed according to the Iraqi sources. [331] The Kurdish forces also repelled an attack by ISIS militants who conduct their attack from Turz Khurmatu, which is under the control of Shia militants.[332]

7.2 The security situation in Kirkuk

Until 2016 it was generally accepted by the Home Office that violence in Kirkuk was at a level that would mean an individual could not return to Kirkuk. Kirkuk is one of the disputed territories and strategically important because of its geographical position with respect to the KRI and its substantial oil reserves that amount to about 12% of the total estimated oil reserves in Iraq. Since the international intervention in Iraq led by the United States in 2003 the Kirkuk governorate has experienced severe violence from various insurgent groups (including Al Qaeda and ISIS). In October 2018, Kirkuk was occupied by Iraqi forces supported by the PMU (Hashd al-Shaabi Shia mlitias), expelling Kurdish officials and armed forces (Peshmerga). When Iraqi forces supported by the PMU occupied Kirkuk, over 150, 000 Kurdish people fled Kirkuk in fear of violence from government forces and militias (although a proportion has since returned). It was reported that the " United Nations voiced concern at reports that civilians, mainly Kurds, were being driven out of parts of northern Iraq retaken by Iraqi forces and their houses and businesses looted and destroyed, and urged Baghdad to stop any such abuses."[333] It remains the case that violence in Kirkuk is endemic. On 31 December 2017 it was reported that gunmen attacked two cafes in Kirkuk. The report stated: "Due to the deteriorating security situation in the province of Kirkuk since the Oct. 16 attack and takeover by Iraqi forces and Iranian-backed Shia Hashd al-Shaabi militias, such incidents are becoming a daily occurrence."[334]

The Danish Immigration Service reported about Kirkuk: "Some of the violence is caused by organised crime, while some of it can have political connotations, and finally some of it can be a combination of both. There are many different groups and conventional and unconventional actors operating in- and outside Kirkuk City. There are no real differences among the ethnic groups when it comes to violence, and criminal activities seem arbitrary and *everybody can be a victim*.[emphasis added]… relations among the ethnic groups are strained, which is the root cause of the violence in Kirkuk. There is a lot of distrust among the different ethnic groups and violent attacks based on hatred and revenge takes place frequently.[335] On 25 January 2018 a bomb went off near a Shia mosque in southern Kirkuk. Again the news report emphasized: "The security situation in Kirkuk has significantly deteriorated since the Iraqi army and Iranian-backed Shia Hashd al-Shaabi militias took over the disputed province from the Peshmerga in October."[336] Similarly it was reported: An Iraqi Federal Police Forces officer was killed in an improvised explosive device attack on a police patrol in a southern suburb of Kirkuk, a security source told Kurdistan 24 on Monday… Since Iraqi forces and the Iranian-backed Hashd al-Shaabi militias took control of Kirkuk, the oil-rich city has experienced unprecedented security incidents including kidnappings, assassinations, and bombings."[337] At the same time there is a resurgence of ISIS (Daesh) in the Kirkuk area with the activation of sleeper cells who are launching attacks and engaging Iraqi forces. More importantly, the occupation by Iraqi forces and the Shia Hashd al-Shaabi militias the local balance of power between different groupings in the Kirkuk area has been destroyed. The Iraqi authorities are involved in Arabisation, forcing Kurds to leave their homes in local villages.[338] The situation in Kirkuk has not improved since the defeat of ISIS in Mosul. This is why the Foreign and Commonwealth Office warns against all travel to the area in its 2019 travel advice.[339]

In February 2019 the was an attack on the Azadi Teaching Hospital in Kirkuk in which a medical practitioner was physically attacked, prompting the WHO to call on the authorities to provide security: "WHO calls on the authorities in Iraq to ensure the safety of health workers, health facilities, and the sanctity of health care," said Dr Adham Rashad Ismail, acting WHO Representative in Iraq. "Such attacks constitute a serious violation of international humanitarian law and deprive the most vulnerable population of children, women and the elderly of their right to essential health services," he added."[340] On 31 May 2019 four people were killed and 15 were injured in four bomb attacks in Kirkuk, demonstrating the persistence of random violence by extremists in the city.[341]

The Iraqi authorities are not capable to properly secure Kirkuk and its neighbouring areas. Thus, it was reported: "Shiwan Dawudi, a member of parliament from Patriotic Union of Kurdistan, says even if IS has lost territory, it is still active. Dawudi told Al-Monitor, "True, IS has lost territory but the organization is still alive, their militants are around. For example, there were 2,000-2,500 armed IS militants in Hawija. But after the liberation of Hawija, about 300 IS militants were captured dead or alive. What happened to the rest? Where did they go? They retreated to the mountains and valleys around Kirkuk. … Some joined sleeper cells and some hid among the people. They reorganized after a few months and resumed operations."[342]

The Kirkuk governorate remains the most violence prone in Iraq, second only to Ninewa. The districts with the highest number of security-related incidents leading to civilian deaths in 2018 were Kirkuk followed by Hawija. The European Asylum Support Office has stated: "Iraq security expert Michael Knights, based on his incident/attack data set and research on security trends, gave the view in late 2018 that ISIL retains 'permanently operating attack cells' in Kirkuk, in districts of Hawija, Rashad, Zab, Dibis, Makhmour, and Ghaeda, in or near Kirkuk province."[343]

The security situation in Northern Iraq fluctuates, and it is important to understand that there is no guarantee that it will improve in the future. Throughout Iraq there are at least 120,000 militant fighters who are part of Shia militias that ostensibly support the Iraqi armed forces, but who are to some extent controlled by the Iranian government and are engaged in criminal enterprises involving kidnapping, extortion and the oppression of Sunni civilians. At the same time ISIS (Daesh) is waging an indiscriminate campaign of violence. In 2019 there is a looming confrontation between Iran and the United States which if it escalates would most likely result in increasing violence in northern Iraq, the Kurdish region, Syria and Lebanon, as indicated by the withdrawal of non-emergency US government employees from Iraq in anticipation of future risks.[344]

7.3 Issues in relation to the threat from ISIS (Daesh) in Kirkuk and the Kurdish Region of Iraq

5.4.1 In 2017, as ISIS was in the process of losing its last territories, the Kurdish commanders became aware that ISIS was regrouping and going into hiding: "As ISIS' so-called caliphate is defeated, intelligence officers and local officials warn the group will turn to guerrilla tactics. A few months ago, intelligence officers and local officials started noticing an increasing stream of ISIS commanders and fighters leaving Mosul and heading into the Hamrin Mountains, Reuters reported on Thursday. The Hamrin Mountains run from the border with Iran, along the southern edge of Kirkuk province, and northwest to the Tigris River. They offer militants hard to locate hideouts as well as easy access to four of Iraq's provinces. Lahur Talabany, director of Kurdistan's counter-terror body, told Reuters in February that … there are signs that ISIS fighters are sheltering in the Hamrin Mountains between Tikrit and Hawija. "It is a very tough terrain. It is very difficult for the Iraqi military to control," he said. "It's a good hideout place and a place they could have access from province to province without getting detected."

Even though the last remains of the territorial caliphate has been eliminated, and President Trump declared victory over ISIS and the withdrawal of US forces from Syria, the fact remains that ISIS is still a potent force in the region. Thus TIME reported: "The most recent UN estimates put the number of ISIS militants in Syria and Iraq today at between 20,000 and 30,000, with most dispersed over territory the group no longer fully controls. That's not many fewer than the 33,000 fighters U.S. intelligence officials estimated the group had at its 2015 peak, according to VOA." [345] A similar assessment was given by the Secretary-General of Interpol: "ISIS fighters retain the expertise, networks and intention to strike at the United States, Jürgen Stock, the secretary-general of Interpol, told NBC News in an exclusive interview at the organization's headquarters in France. "The threat is still very acute, the threat is complex, and the threat is more international than ever," Stock said. "[346]Likewise the US Director of National Security Dan Coates that ISSI remains a potent force in Syria and Iraq: ""ISIS still commands thousands of fighters in Iraq and Syria, and it maintains eight branches, more than a dozen networks, and thousands of dispersed supporters around the world, despite significant leadership and territorial losses," reads the Worldwide Threat Assessment, released by Director of National Intelligence Dan Coats on Tuesday."[347] According to the Danish Immigration Service: "After its military defeat and loss of territory control, ISIS has evolved to be a more ordinary insurgent group in a more traditional sense. The group is especially concentrated in places such as the Hamreen Mountains and Hawija, Kirkuk Governorate, but also in Diyala and Ninewa Governorates as well as in the border area between Iraq and Syria. According to Institute for the Study of War (ISW), ISIS has also established a support zone along the Iraqi- Iranian border that it is used as a base for operations into Iran. ISIS remnants (including the Kurdish Salafi- Jihadist group Ansar al-Islam) have maintained a support zone in the Halabja Mountains in KRI since late 2016. The same source notes that local Kurdish forces have detained numerous alleged cells in Sulaymaniyah Governorate in Northern Iraq since January 2018." [348]

With respect to Erbil in particular and the KRG in general, the Department of State issued the following report on the risks of terrorism in the region in its 2019 report: "There is serious risk from terrorism in Erbil. Although ISIS no longer holds physical territory, the group has shown resilience. Remaining ISIS elements have transitioned to recruitment, fundraising, and insurgency operations. ISIS maintains lethal capabilities and presents a serious threat almost anywhere along the 700 mile-long Peshmerga and Iraqi Army defensive line.

Throughout Ninewa and Kirkuk provinces, ISIS frequently carries out asymmetric attacks, to include the use of vehicle-borne improvised explosive devices (VBIEDs), ambushes, small unit infantry-style assaults, and assassinations. Terrorists often target Iraqi and Western civilians, Iraqi security forces, Kurdistan regional security forces, the Government of Iraq and the Kurdistan Regional Government (KRG).

Although on the defensive, ISIS still remains capable and extremely dangerous. On 23 July 2018 ISIS militants mounted an attacked on the Erbil governorate, a very bold operation against the central power of the regional authorities.[349] Recent reporting indicates that ISIS maintains sleeper cells in the western portion of Mosul. ISIS remnants constitute a threat to Westerners operating in or traversing Mosul and traveling west toward Tal Afar and Sinjar. In July 2018, three Erbil-based ISIS militants attacked and occupied Erbil's governorate building, holding hostages and killing one civilian employee during a five-hour standoff. IKR security forces killed all three attackers at the scene. Authorities arrested an Erbil-based imam in connection to the attack; he later declared his allegiance to ISIS and confessed to planning the attack and recruiting the three teenage gunmen. In October 2018, Kurdish counterterrorism forces arrested several ISIS financiers in a series of raids in Erbil, lending credence to the continued presence and ongoing threats presented by ISIS within the city. "[350]

In April 2019, Kurdistan Regional Security Council Chancellor Masrour Barzani noted the concern about the rising number of ISIS attacks.[351] While the central figures and buildings of the Kurdish Regional Government are well protected, it cannot be said that this extends to ordinary persons who would targets for ISIS for some reason or other. Thus, it was reported in July 2018: "Over the past two months, dozens of people, including local government officials, tribal elders and village chiefs, have been abducted and killed or ransomed by fighters claiming affiliation with the Islamic State. Electricity infrastructure and oil pipelines have been blown up. Armed men dressed as security forces and manning fake checkpoints have hijacked trucks and robbed travellers, rendering the main Baghdad-Kirkuk highway unsafe for a period of weeks." In January 2019 it was reported: "People from surrounding areas of Diyala's city of Khanaqin have abandoned their villages and moved to safer towns as the number of the Islamic State-claimed attacks have considerably increased, witnesses reported on Wednesday. Over the past 16 days, Islamic State members have carried out 10 attacks around the areas of Khanaqin and Jalawla, targeting Iraqi federal police forces and villagers."[352] As the number of attacks is now escalating in the region, it is not plausible to suggest that individuals can be effectively protected by the security forces or Iraq and the KRG. As the authorities have no idea where the extremists are hiding exactly, or whom they intend to target, it is impractical to suggest that effective protection can exist. Given that ISIS recruits include members of the security services, there is a serious risk to anyone who lives in an area targeted by ISIS, or persons that ISIS targets individually.

The Kirkuk area remains an epicentre of violence. Thus, the Center for International Studies in Washington, a leading think tank, reported:" Through October 2018, Islamic State attacks in Kirkuk province have more than doubled from 2017 to 2018."[353] In the recent past ISIS (Daesh) has been able to carry out attacks in Erbil and there is no evidence that there is any area in Iraq (including the KRG) where attacks from Daesh cannot occur, or where Daesh has no influence given that it has gone underground. Refugees from other parts of Iraq will not only face the risk of violence, but also may not be able to enter the KRI as they is not from the KRI, they have no guarantor, lack the necessary documentation and will face substantial difficulties obtaining accommodation or employment given the current security, social and economic upheavals of the region.[354]

Some asylum seekers fear that they will be persecuted and at risk of harm due to a family member's (usually the father's) links to the Ba'ath Party for which this family member was killed. The background to this issue is that during the Anfal campaign (1986-89) against the Kurds the Iraqi government under Saddam Hussein manipulated local allegiance using National Defence Battalions, militia units with military and security duties active mostly in the Kurdish region. The Kurds referred to them dismissively as "jash" or "donkeys". The persons appointed by the government to recruit the "jash" were tribal leaders or other officials known as "mustashars" (advisors) who received money for each recruit. The mustashar supported the campaign against their own people because of local tribal rivalries or because of the pay they received.[355] In the course of the campaign there were mass killings, the use of conventional weapons as well as chemical weapons against the civilian population.

According to a study by Sarah Brown: "The *mustashar* system strengthened the political and economic position of certain tribal leaders as well as contributing to rivalries between tribal groups, though some *mustashars* managed to raise troops without a tribal base, profiting economically in the process."[356]

'The Iraqi government that went through a process of de-Baathification and many high-ranking former members of the Baath Party have been persecuted, including death penalties for the most senior members believes that the KRG is "harboring former Baathists and collaborators in their crimes. Armed Kurdish groups consisting of tens of thousands of fighters, known as the Light Regiments, joined the Baath regime in its numerous crimes against the Kurdish people in the 1970s and 1980s."[357] Moreover: "Websites close to former Prime Minister Nouri al-Maliki accused the KRG of harboring a large number of Baathists persecuted in Baghdad and of using this as leverage during negotiations on contentious matters, leading to objections among the Kurds. Sot Kurdistan newspaper said in this regard that Erbil has turned into "a hotbed for the former and new Baathists."[358]

The KRG authorities have denied these allegations. It is clear that the presence of alleged collaborators with the Saddam regime in the KRG, former Ba'ath party members or militia members ("jash", "mustashar") is a very sensitive political issue. There are lists of Kurds that collaborated with the regime in the Anfal campaign. If an individual is identified as a close relative of a member of the Baath party, he/she is at risk of being either arrested and mistreated or refused entry into the KRG.

Given the atrocities committed by the Iraqi government under Saddam Hussein against the Kurds, it is plausible that there would be non-state actors in Northern Iraq and the Kurdish region that would persecute known members of the Baa'th Party and their family. Many people also have fallen victim to attacks from terrorists and/or militias in the context of the general security situation in the region.

Persons who come from Kirkuk or other areas previously under the control of the KRG cannot always return to the KRI since they are not from the KRI and therefore formally they cannot be deported to the KRI. The recent country guidance case stated evidence required to obtain as CSID (an identity document needed to enter the KRI and to obtain accommodation and employment): "Having contacted the consulate in London, and checked on the website of the Iraqi embassy in Sweden, Dr Fatah states that the authorities will require the applicant to first make a statement explaining why he needs a CSID and attach this to his application form, which must countersigned by the head of the applicant's family and stamped by the consulate or embassy; he must then produce his Iraqi passport and proof of status in the country where he is applying, the name of a representative (proxy) in Iraq, an additional form completed by the head of the applicant's family verifying that the contents of his application form were true, four colour copies of his INC, and 10 colour photographs. Crucially the applicant must be able to produce something which can establish the location of his family's details in the civil register. This should be a CSID, an INC or birth certificate. If none of these are available to the applicant he must supply the identity documents of his parents."[359] It is quite clear therefore that many individuals will not be able to obtain the required documentation and cannot be returned to the KRI. This applies particularly to persons from Kirkuk which was previously governed by the KRG but is not part of the KRI and therefore they cannot be returned to the KRI.

The 2018 Country Guidance Case cited additional evidence: "The private rental market presents its own difficulties. Dr Fatah considered it to be inconceivable that an individual returnee would find it possible to rent a room from a family in what he called a 'traditional' neighbourhood. The accommodation in these old residential areas is designed for large families. A man on his own with no contacts would be viewed with suspicion and as a matter of honour families would not have him in the house where there would be young women of marriageable age. As such what we would think of in the UK as 'lodging' would not be culturally acceptable; it simply does not happen. If a family defied convention to take in a lodger who was a stranger, Dr Fatah predicts that the family themselves would be ostracised. A single woman on her own would be regarded as even stranger."[360] While male returnees to the KRI might be able to find apartments if they could put down sufficient money, even this would not be possible without a CSID. Moreover, employment would not be available with a CSID and the evidence cited by the Home Office states that the unemployment rate for IDPs in the KRI is 70%.

Whether or not a person could obtain a CSID in the embassy depends on whether he has the required documentation (i.e. a passport or the book and registration number of his family registration details). In practice, if he has no passport it is unlikely that he will be able obtain the CSID in the embassy. As a result of the intense fighting in the past and the current level of violence in Northern Iraq as well as the risks of travel from Baghdad, especially trying to pass through multiple checkpoints without a CSID, it may not be possible for an individual to travel to his/her home governorate and even he/she could travel there it may not be possible to obtain a CSID from an area formerly occupied by ISIS (Daesh). Although there are Civil Affairs Offices in Baghdad that can be accessed by persons from other parts of Iraq, it may not have the information required to issue a CSID given that the Kurdish Region experienced a long period after the Gulf War when there was a Kurdish uprising followed by a civil conflict in the Kurdish region and local records were destroyed during the occupation of ISIS of Northern Iraq and the confident statements by the Home Office about the availability of a CSID are not confirmed by experience on the ground.[361] For a long time the Home Office claimed that there was a "nationality court" in Baghdad where a person could have their nationality confirmed, but it turned out this was a misunderstanding that arose from expert testimony during a tribunal and there is no such institution. A report on mobility in Iraq stated: "During the conflict period with ISIL, there were frequent cases of missing or lost civil identification due to fleeing or destruction of homes. Many Iraqis who lived in ISIL areas lost one or more of their pieces of civil documentation or had them confiscated by ISIL or were issued with documents from IS unrecognised by the government. The UN estimated in 2016 that as many as 50 % of displaced families had at least one family member missing essential civil identity documents. MRG's 2016 research report on IDPs from Ninewa and Anbar found that 78 % of the more than 50 IDPs interviewed, mostly Anbaris who had been displaced to Baghdad, had encountered difficulties re-obtaining civil documentation linking this to high illiteracy and exacerbated by communal suspicion of Arab Sunnis from former IS areas (89). Landinfo stated that internally displaced people frequently require assistance to re-obtain their national ID card if they live elsewhere than where they are registered as ID cards are issued in their home district according DIS/Landinfo wrote in November 2018 that the lack of civil documentation for functioning in Iraqi society is a 'major obstacle' for IDPs to return."[362] Persons who do not have the required documentation, may be unable to obtain a CSID and if returned to Iraq he would be internally displaced persons (IDP).

7.4 Honour crimes and blood feuds

As in other Middle Eastern countries, tribal disputes, blood feuds and honour killings are part of the regional culture. An *honour killing* is the murder of a member of a family or social group by other members, based on the belief of the perpetrators that the victim has brought dishonour upon the family or community. Honour killings are directed mostly against women and girls but have been extended to men and can escalate to homicidal feuds between families or even tribes. Honour killings are very common in Middle Eastern and South Asian countries and take various forms. For example, it is common for husband's estranged or divorced from their wives or prospective husbands who have been rejected to commit or seek to commit violent acts against the women concerned, including murder (honour killings).[363] In the United Kingdom there are numerous women in safe houses provided for by social services who have been attacked or threatened by their husbands or other relatives.[364] For the most part, honour killings in Muslim countries are related to unapproved relationships or refusals to marry a designated partner, or for inappropriate or "Western" demeanour and behaviour. In Pakistan honour killings, are known as karo-kari, often find support in Pakistani society, especially in rural areas. It is estimated that there more than 10,000 honour killings in Pakistan every year. The concepts of honour are very deeply entrenched in the culture of the

Muslim countries, and the authorities mostly ignore the killing or maiming of women by their families. If the perpetrators are prosecuted the sentences are often light in relation to the offense.[365] The killing of a family member is a serious affront to honour that can give rise to a campaign of revenge.

In Iraq honour killings are widespread and remain a serious problem.[366] As a report from the Foreign and Commonwealth Office stated: "Domestic violence and 'honour' killing remain a problem in Iraq. Thousands of Iraqi women are beaten or killed each year. Some NGOs in the Kurdistan region of Iraq offer shelters for women escaping violence. However, such shelters operate in an undefined legal framework..."[367] Honour killings are also common in Iran, they occur in all parts of society but more commonly occur among more conservative tribal peoples such as Kurdish, Lori, Arab, Baluchi and Turkish-speaking tribes. [368]

Like in other Middle Eastern countries, there is a significant degree of cultural acceptance and support for the concept of honour killings and public law permits judges to mitigate sentences, if need there is even any prosecution. According to the United States Department and the UNHCR honour killings are prevalent in all parts of the country. According to Amnesty International:

"The regime of honour is unforgiving: women on whom suspicion has fallen are not given an opportunity to defend themselves, and family members have no socially acceptable alternative but to remove the stain on their honour by attacking the woman. "[369]

Article 409 of the Iraqi penal code provides for leniency in the case of honour killings, mandating a maximum of three years in prison for a man who kills his wife or other close female relative *and her partner* after discovering them in the act of adultery and deprives the victims of the right to self-defence in such situations. According to Article 130 of the penal code sentences as low as six months. The rate of honour killings soared in Iraq after 2003. Of 81 such killings recorded in Basra in 2008, only five resulted in the perpetrators being convicted, but many offenses are never recorded. Indeed, those who commit honour killings often find the policy sympathetic or even encouraging, as the perception that they are doing the right thing finds a high degree of acceptance in society. Perpetrators are often released without charge or further investigation.

The occurrence of killings in the context of defending "honour" was emphasized by a fact-finding mission by a Danish Immigration Service that reported about "Honour Crimes against men in the Kurdistan Region of Iraq". Indeed, it goes as far as stating that men and women are equally at risk of being victims of honour crimes and that honour crimes against men are common in the Kurdish region of Iraq. Wrong-doing against honour is considered unforgivable and the concern about wrong-doing against a family honour does not diminish over the years. This was confirmed by various leading representatives from local organisations, who all stated that unless an honour dispute is resolved, it will remain and can give rise to violence at any time. For example: "Ari Rafiq and Huda S. Zangana, … Erbil, stated the risk of retribution for an honour-related offense is always there. The matter of a tarnished honour of a family not yet rectified is eternal, and if a lasting reconciliation is not accomplished, the offender of that family honour will be at risk at all times. Even if a man responsible for threats against a person who has offended his family's honour is imprisoned, there is a serious risk that another member of the offended family will undertake the revenge, including the killing of the offender."[370] The border between Iran and Iraq does not codify a difference in culture between Kurds on both sides of the border and the statements about Kurds in Iraq equally apply to Kurds in Iran.[371]

Hassan Berwari, Diakonia, Dahuk, stated in his response to the questions by a Danish investigating team that although there are laws in Kurdish Iraq dealing with the issue of honour crimes in the Kurdish Region of Iraq, ordinary people are looking to tribal leaders rather than the authorities (police and courts) in settling any disputes. This is evidently due to the fact that it is difficult to either obtain protection or satisfaction from the authorities.

Reconciliation without recourse to violence is almost impossible if the parties belong to different tribes.

"Mahdi M. Qadr and Fakhir Ibrahim, PAO, Erbil, stated that occasionally a settlement between the families involved, could include an agreement to kill the daughter and the son of the respective families. Hoshyar S. Malo, KHRW, Erbil, explained that two heads of tribes may decide that the two families involved in an incident where a family's honour has been tainted, should kill their son and daughter respectively. The solution involving a family agreeing to kill their own son themselves is not unusual, as this prevents more "blood" between the tribes. By killing their own son, the family "cuts the blood" and prevents more blood from flowing between the tribes. Settling honour issues often involves marriage, however, it is not always the case that this can be accepted which subsequently can lead to more serious settlements involving killing."[372] This account of conflicts involving different tribes shows that there is a real possibility of violence over honour disputes, such a risk also exists in disputes over honour between families of the same tribe or within the same family.

More than 12,000 women were killed in the name of honour in Kurdistan from 1991 to 2007, according to Aso Kamal of the Doaa Network Against Violence.[373] The numbers have reduced to some extent since then and the Kurdish government officially treats honour killings as murders, but nevertheless social attitudes have no changed and the practice continued as Islamic leaders opposed the government's disapproval of practice. It remains widely approved of and for this reason the authorities cannot be relied on to protect the victims as even those working in the security services and judicial system share the same values. Honour killings are often disguised as suicides. These often take the form of women setting themselves on fire (self-immolation). [374]

Revenge is a very central aspect of Middle Eastern culture. Revenge killings are very common throughout Iraq, including the Kurdish area, and although not legally sanctioned are carried out by individuals, families, tribal representatives and even soldiers or other persons representing authorities.[375] A factfinding mission from the Danish Refugee Council considered the possibility of protection from the authorities: "According to UNHCR, there is very little regard of law enforcement among the local population in KRI and people do not make use of the police or the courts. UNHCR said that the courts are not seen to respond, even though, in principle, they have a number of excellent laws meeting international standards. In addition, UNHCR explained that access to rule of law is dependent on ethnic and religious affiliation, tribe, connections, family and relatives, and it is very difficult, if not impossible, for an individual to stand up for his rights by himself."[376]

As for potential victims of an honour crime: "Journalist Osama Al Habahbeh said that the only way to protect a woman who risks honour killing is to put her in jail or a shelter resembling a jail where she risks being raped or sold through human trafficking by the authorities."[377] The Danish Refugee Council report also states: "In line with this, UNHCR stated that, in KRI, it would be difficult for a victim of an honour crime to escape the perpetrators and seek protection from the authorities. Journalist Osama Al Habahbeh said that a woman fleeing honour killing cannot hide anywhere in Iraq."[378]

In the regional culture, it would be strictly forbidden for a woman to have a relationship with a man without knowledge or permission of the family. Many Muslim families consider it completely unacceptable for a male person to be in the company of a female person if the two are not related or not married. Without a doubt the family would have questioned the girlfriend until she gave the relevant information about the unknown man.

For potential victims of an honour killing, protection from the police and authorities cannot be relied upon, despite efforts by the government to deal with these practices, as a result of the general problems with the manner in which the judicial system and police operate and attitudes among the police and courts to honour killings. Potential victims are at risk of actions taken in revenge by the family who may seek to persecute the in order to assuage their sense of grievance and violation of family honour.

7.5 Summary: Iraq, a dangerous country

It is evident that Iraq remains a very dangerous country, having experienced success waves of severe violence due to the invasion and the insurgencies, the rise and fall of the Islamic State (ISIS/Daesh), and the Popular Mobilization Force (Shi'a Militias). Iraq is essentially a country divided into three, with central Iraq under very considerable Iranian influence that does not promote stability, democracy or the rule of law. There is also considerable violence in the Kurdish Region even though UK authorities consider it safe. The large number of internally displaced persons, the military and criminal actions of 120,000 fighters in militias and the prevalence of ISIS/Daesh sleeper cells and underground fighters means that there remain very considerable risks to security and to individual safety in Iraq

PART III
Iran

CHAPTER 8

Human Rights Issues in Iran

8.1 Iran's treatment of dissenters

Iran is a country in which political dissent is considered to be a form of criminal activity that is actively suppressed with the use of the criminal law, Individuals may be subject to arbitrary arrest, torture and incarceration. Individuals belonging to minorities in Iran, who are believed to number about half of the population of about 70 million, are subject to an array of discriminatory laws and practices. These include land and property confiscations, denial of state employment under the Gozinesh (selection) criteria and restrictions on social, cultural, linguistic and religious freedoms which often result in other human rights violations such as political prisoners, unfair trials of political prisoners before Revolutionary Courts, physical punishment and use of the death penalty, as well as restrictions on movement and denial of other civil rights.[379] Amnesty International in relation to the post-election demonstrations reports that: 'During the widespread unrest that followed the contested election result in June 2009, thousands of people were arbitrarily arrested, dozens were killed on the streets or died in detention, and many said they were tortured or otherwise ill-treated.'[380] Reports indicates that since 2005, the human rights situation there has dramatically worsened.[381] In the aftermath of the Iranian elections on June 12, 2009 the human rights situation has deteriorated even further. Torture, systematic arrests, and imprisonment are common occurrences. Iran currently has the distinction of having the world's highest record of public hangings and executions.[382] Ahmadinejad raised the number of executions from 86 in 2005, when he took office as president for the first time to 346 in 2008. During the short period between the June elections and the inauguration of Ahmadinejad in August 2009, 115 people were executed. According to a report from Amnesty International, there were 196 executions in Iran in the first half of 2009. By November 2009, there have been 359 executions.[383]

According to the Universal Periodic Review of the Human Rights Council 'the practice of torture is widespread'. The Medical Foundation for the Care of Victims of Tortures reports that: 'Torture, organised violence and sexual assault by the authorities is nothing new in Iran'.[384] World Report 2011 on the situation of human rights and torture in Iran maintains that: Authorities systematically used torture to coerce confessions. Student activist Abdullah Momeni wrote to Supreme Leader Ayatollah Seyed Ali Khamenei in September describing the torture he suffered at the hands of jailers. At this writing no high-level official has been prosecuted for the torture, ill treatment, and deaths of three detainees held at Kahrizak detention centre after June 2009.[385]

If a person is arrested, according to Refugee Review Tribunal Australia the accused normally has an opportunity to post a "bond" or bail to maintain their freedom pending their trial. 'There are different methods of obtaining a bail. Bail can be obtained through a surety, through providing security or through a cash deposit. Under Islamic law, for minor offences, the accused can be released on his own bail.' The report adds that 'where the accused fails to appear, he can be tried in this absence.'[386] Article 140 of the Law of Criminal Procedure of Iran states that 'failure of the person released on bail to surrender himself at the appointed time, results in forfeiture of the security.' In some cases the accused could be asked to report to the Police daily, weekly or monthly. According to the UK's Asylum and Immigration Tribunal report in 2009: Events in Iran following the 12 June 2009 presidential elections have led to a government crackdown on persons seen to be opposed to the present government and the Iranian judiciary has become even less independent. Persons who are likely to be perceived by the authorities in Iran as being actively associated with protests against the June 12 election results may face a real risk of persecution or ill treatment, although much will depend on the particular circumstances.

Being a part of a protest movement such as the Green Movement in Iran has severe consequences. Since June 2009 anyone who has supported the Green Movement is considered as a threat for the Iranian government national security. There are a large number of Iranians who were arrested in demonstrations for the Green Movement. For example, any action related to the election of 1388 or Mr Mosavi's presidential campaign has been considered to constitute a crime.

For example, Shahnaz Akmali lost her son (Mostafa Karim Beygi) in one of the protests against election results of 2009. She was just attending peaceful protest in Tehran. Her son was shot in Tehran in a religious ceremony (Ashura)[387]. After the autopsy it was clear that he was shot in his forehead. The family received his body but was not allowed to hold any funeral and they had to bury him in a village around Tehran at night very quietly. His mother participated in a protest, a few people (in plain clothes) went to her house early in the morning and moved her to an unknown location. It is not clear if she was arrested by the intelligence ministry or revolutionary guard in Iran.[388]

As an indication of the nature and extent of persecution by the government of people who were in favour of Green Movement there is a list of names of some who lost their lives in protests against the result of 2009 elections:

Nasser Amirnejad was a 24-year-old student at the Research and Science university and was shot. [389]

Mehdi Karami was a 25-year- old student who was shot and killed.[390]

Ashkan Sohrabi was a 20 years old computer student who was shot three times in his chest.[391]

Sohrab Arabi who was arrested in June 2009 for objecting to the result of presidential election, he was supposed to be released by the Court. For almost a month his mom was waiting in Enghelab Court every afternoon to see her son. However, in July 2009 she was offered a collection of photos of people who were dead killed to recognize her son.[392]

Neda Aghasoltan was shot in one of the protests in Iran.[393]

Mostafa Ghanian was shot just because he went on the roof shouting "ALLAHO AKBAR" (it was a method of showing unhappiness and objections to the result of election) which means "God is great". [394]

Mohesn Roholamini was arrested while protesting in 2009 and imprisoned in Kahrizak detention centre.[395] He was severely beaten in the prison and seriously injured. A few days after he was imprisoned, he was supposed to be transferred to another prison but on the way, due to his critical condition and injuries, he passed away.[396]

Mostafa Kiarostami was 22 years old. He was hit and injured in Tehran, he called his mother to ask for help, his mother took him home and learned he was in a critical condition so she took him to a hospital but it was too late.[397]

Kianoosh Asa was a 25 year old who disappeared during protests in favour of the Green Movement and his dead body was delivered to his family.[398]

Hossein Akbari was a 16-year-old student and was killed after protests in 2009 against the result of presidential election. However, his family did not know where he was until they received a phone call and were asked to go to Emam Khomieni hospital to receive their son's body.[399]

Given the fact that the rule of law is compromised in Iran for political purposes and when it comes to politics anyone can be penalized for alleged anti-government activities whether they participated in them or not.

Most of the time according to the Islamic rule, people who are part of the Green Movement and activists will be dealt with on the basis of two articles of the law which are 498 and 512. However, these numbers refer to Islamic law and in the Iranian state penal code the relevant paragraphs of the criminal code are 498, 499 and 500.[400]

According to article 498 whoever with any faith, alone or with more than two people inside or outside of the county establishes a group or guide a group with the purpose of putting in danger the country's security will be recognized as a person who is at war with god and will be sentenced to two to 10 years imprisonment.[401]

According to article 499 whoever is a member of the above mentioned groups (the groups mentioned in article 498) will be imprisoned from three months to five years unless they can prove they did not know anything about the intention of the group or did not know they are becoming a part of the group.[402]

Article 500 indicates whoever is deemed to oppose the Iranian government or cooperates with any foreign organization which is against the Islamic Republic of Iran will be sentenced to imprisonment from 3 months to one year.[403] The lawful punishments are indicated in the above paragraphs and anyone related to the Green Movement will be punished according to those articles. There has been an increase of intolerance for groups that identify with the armed or military opposition and if someone is identified as belonging to such groups, he or she would likely be interrogated and imprisoned. Anyone involved in the Green Movement will be charged with will be crimes against the Islamic Republic of Iran, insulting the Supreme Leader and collusion.[404] Apart from the articles of the penal code which referred to above other relevant articles are 514 and 610. Article 514 is about any insult to Imam Khomeini who was the founder of Iranian revolution.[405]

According to article of 514 whoever insults Imam Khomeini or the Supreme Leader just by words will be sentenced to imprisonment from 6 months to two years depending on the judge.[406] According to article 610 whenever two people form a group with the purpose of acting against the Iranian government they will be sentenced to imprisonment from two years to five years.[407] Whoever was a part of Green Movement at any part of time can be subject to prosecution for all the mentioned crimes bearing in mind that the Iranian government has recorded and registered whatever has happened before, during and after the presidential election in 2009.[408]

Activists of the Green Movement live in fear in Iran.[409] The risk upon return depends on the visibility of the individual both online and offline. If someone is not visible enough, they may initially escape persecution, however it is not possible to say that they will not be at risk because often the authorities act rather arbitrarily. Even people who are not high-profile activists are arrested and prosecuted upon return to Iran for minor political activities that they have engaged in online while being outside of Iran or in Iran prior to leaving the country.

People who related to the Green Movement have released their stories in international media that how they left the country in terror and left their families and loved ones behind.[410] The exact number of people who were killed or arrested is unknown. The Green Movement it is also mentioned in the Iranian new website kalame.[411] There is a video clip of the Iranian families who lost their family member in demonstrations against the result of presidential election in 2009.[412]

According to the Iranian Minorities Human Right Organisation, the family of an Iranian political refugee, Habib Nabgan, have been unlawfully arrested and detained by the Iranian government. The reports says that, his wife Ma'soumeh Ka'bi, and their five children have been told to pressure him into handing himself over to the Islamic regime. The report adds that it is common behaviour to arrest and punish the family of the accused when they cannot find the accused himself/herself.[413] According to Amnesty International: 'Ma'soumeh Ka'bi and her five children are prisoners of conscience, held solely in order to force Habib Nabgan to give himself up to the Iranian authorities.'[414] Elsewhere Amnesty International in regards to the similar cases reports that:

Soghra Khudayrawi and her four-year-old son Zeidan were reportedly arrested in Ahwaz on March 7. Her husband, Khalaf Derhab Khudayrawi, is said to be wanted by the authorities in connection with his political activities, Amnesty said. Sakina Naisi, a mother of five, was reportedly arrested in Ahwaz on February 27 along with her 19-year-old son Nahez and taken to the Sepidar detention centre. Nahez was reportedly released after about 10 days in detention. Sakina Naisi is three months pregnant and reportedly suffers from asthma, the statement added. Her husband, Ahmad Naisi, a prominent political activist, is said to be wanted by the authorities. Following Sakina Naisi's arrest, the Iranian authorities reportedly destroyed her husband's family home in the Shoaybiyeh district of Ahwaz with bulldozers. Amnesty International believes all five are very likely to be prisoners of conscience held solely in order to force their husbands and fathers to give themselves up to the Iranian authorities.[415]

According to Joe Stork, Middle East director at Human Rights Watch, 'Iran's repressive system of controlling people's dress, behaviour, and personal lives violates fundamental rights.' This reports adds that private houses in Iran are raided frequently for different reasons by the security forces.[416]

The Human Rights Watch World Report 2011 on the situation of human rights in Iran states that, Iran's human rights crisis deepened as the government sought to consolidate its power following the disputed presidential election in 2009. Public demonstrations waned after security forces used live ammunition to suppress protesters in late 2009, resulting in the death of at least seven protesters. Authorities announced that security forces had arrested more than 6,000 individuals after June 2009. Hundreds—including lawyers, rights defenders, journalists, civil society activists, and opposition leaders—remain in detention without charge. Since the election crackdown last year, well over a thousand people have fled Iran to seek asylum in neighbouring countries. Interrogators used torture to extract confessions, on which the judiciary relied on to sentence people to long prison terms and even death. Restrictions on freedom of expression and association, as well as religious and gender-based discrimination, continued unabated.[417]

8.2 Kurdish Iranian refugees in Iraq

During the Iran-Iraq war in the 1980s around 23,000 Iranians fled to Iraq. These included some 16, 000 of Iranian Kurds fled to Iraq. Some refugees came from the towns in the border areas that were destroyed or occupied by Iraq. Some came for political reasons; they were members of Iranian Kurdish opposition groups such as the Democratic Party of Iranian Kurdistan (PDKI).[418] Since the Iran-Iraq War about 30,000 Kurdish Iranians have entered the KRI as migrant workers. There are many Kurdish Iranians living in the KRI without any legal status or permission to reside and work. The Iranian Kurdish refugees came to Iraq during the Iran-Iraq War refugees were all relocated to the Al-Tash Refugee Camp, in Al-Anbar Province 145 km west of Baghdad (not in the KRI).[419]

After the US-led invasion of Iraq and the fall of the Baath regime led by Saddam Hussein in 2003 the refugees based in Anbar province were moved to the Suleimaniyah Governorate in the KRI, These refugees either lived in rented accommodation or were placed in the Kawa Refugee Camp near Erbil and the Barika Refugee Camp near Suleimaniyah.[420]

The issue of ID cards for the Iranian refugees is complicated and has not been handled in a consistent manner in the KRI or by the Government of Iraq. The Danish Immigration Service investigated this matter and reported as follows: "The Kawa Camp Council and the Kawa Camp Committee (hereafter "the Kawa camp representatives") stated that the refugees in Kawa camp do not hold Iraqi residence cards, but only KRG ID cards and UNHCR refugee registration cards. Refugees holding UNHCR refugee registration cards can travel throughout Iraq; the KRG ID card does not permit the refugees to travel freely within Iraq... All Iranian refugees in Al-Tash were initially provided with an Iraqi ID card, but these ID cards were taken from them by UNHCR when they moved to Kawa Refugee Camp in KRI. Instead they were given a UNHCR refugee registration card and a KRG ID card was issued for each family, not for each individual as before. The result is that all the members of each family are dependent on each other when they wish to travel unless they make a copy of the ID but this is illegal. The camp representatives stated that each individual should be issued an ID card. When asked if all adult refugees are issued their own individual KRG ID card the camp representatives explained that all Iranian refugees above the age of 18 have been issued a personal KRG ID card. Concerning residence in KRI the spokesmen for Iranian refugees in Barika Refugee Camp explained that the refugees in Barika camp only have temporary residence permits. The permit, which is an ID for refugees, is to be renewed every six months. In addition, the refugees also hold UNHCR refugee registration cards. Only persons above 18 years of age will get an ID card. Minors are registered in their parents ID card."[421] It is clear from the report that different authorities in different locations applied different policies with regard to ID Cards.

Iranian refugees were given access to PDS cards which gives them access to food rations but this is problematic because the supply of rations is often delayed or sometimes fails entirely. Some critical foods such as flour and rice are not always of a good quality or sufficient quantity.

The Kurdish Iranian refugees in Iraq have been denied Iraqi citizenship. The Kurdish Regional Government has made it clear that according to the constitution of Iraq they do not have the authority to grant citizenship to anyone.[422] This authority resides with the Government of Iraq based in Baghdad. For political reasons, including the fact that the Kurds are considered a minority in Iran that is hostile to the Shia Islamic Republic, the Government of Iraq is not prepared to grant citizenship to the Iranian Kurdish Refugees in Iraq.

The citizenship dilemma faced by Iranian Kurdish refugees in Iraq has been described in the report from the Danish Immigration Service: "According to Sarbast Tawfiq, Mayor of District Qushtapa, the main problems for the Iranian refugees are that they can neither return to Iran, nor obtain Iraqi citizenship, or be resettled in a third country. UNHCR has tried a couple of times to make the Iranian authorities guarantee the safety of the refugees if they go back to Iran, but no guarantee has so far been given. On the other hand, the GoI has not yet been willing to grant citizenship to the Iranian refugees because GoI has no interest in increasing the number of Kurdish citizens in Iraq by granting citizenship to refugees of Kurdish origin. In addition Western countries are not disposed to receive Iranian refugees in Iraq for resettlement. "[423]

8.3 Issues face by non-Muslims in Iran

The Islamic Republic of Iran has pursued a deliberate policy of intolerance towards minority groups and in particular has engaged in the systematic of persecution of religious minorities. This section looks at the issues faced by Baha'i and Christians in Iran. Since 1979 Baha'is in particular have been the victims of a deliberate government policy of persecution and in the first decade after the Islamic revolution more than 200 Baha'is have been killed, hundreds more were imprisoned and tortured. Bahai's have lost their jobs by the tens of thousands, and have been denied access to education and experienced severe discrimination due to their religious beliefs.[424]

The Iranian government has responded to statements by the European Union and the US State Department on the persecution of the Baha'i saying that Baha'is are enemies of the state. In other words, they are considered a political threat, alleged to have been supporters of the former Shah's government and spies employed by the West.[425] This is of course a very common tactics in discrediting a minority group. The Ayatollah Khomeini, even while in exile in France before his return to Iran declared in an interview that the Baha'is were traitors — Zionists — and enemies of Islam.[426] Between 1982 and 1984 the Iranian representative at the United Nations attempted several times to persuade the diplomatic community at the United Nations that the Baha'i Faith was not a legitimate religion like Judaism, Christianity and Zoroastrianism. Indeed it is not acknowledged in Iran that the Baha'i Faith is a religion at all. Instead the Iranian government describes it as a political organization that has engaged in criminal activism against the government of Iran.[427] These accusations by the Iranian government were robustly countered by the United Nations and it was pointed out that if Iran were to acknowledge the fact that the Baha'i Faith is a religion "it would be an admission that freedom of religion does not apply to all in Iran and that it is not abiding by the Universal Declaration of Human Rights and International Covenants on Human Rights to which it is a signatory."[428]

In the last ten years the government persecution of the Baha'i, the largest non-Muslim religious minority in Iran, has substantially intensified. The entire leadership group serving the Baha'i was arrested in 2008 and in 2010 sentenced to 20 years in prison.[429] In 2015 there were widespread protest events to commemorate the seventh year of the imprisonment of the leadership group. Baha'i in Iran live under the constant threat of raids, arrests, detention.[430]

Baha'i in Iran suffer from severe economic discrimination, their rights to education have been curtailed, they are not permitted to assemble and worship. The government controlled media constantly put out propaganda against Baha'i who also are at serious risk from attacks on their persons or properties from people who want to harm them. Such attacks are not prosecuted or punished. Baha'i properties have been subjected to arson attacks and vandalism.

For example, there were reports on raids in Abadeh in October 2013: "Following raids on 14 Baha'i homes in the Iranian city of Abadeh on 13 October 2013, government agents summoned the occupants for questioning and urged them to leave town or face possible deadly attacks from city residents. Agents from the Shiraz office of the Ministry of Intelligence, with agents from Abadeh, launched the raids at about 8 am on 13 October 2013. The homes were searched, and Baha'i books, CDs, computers, and other items, including photographs, were confiscated. During questioning, several Baha'is were told that local residents "don't like you" and that "when you are on the street, they might attack you and your children with knives." But all evidence says the hate is instigated by the Government; Abadeh residents have good relations with Baha'is."[431]

The situation has not improved despite the election of a more reformist president. As Elliott Abrams from the Council on Foreign Relations in the United States reported: "The regime continues to deny the Baha'i rights all other citizens hold. A long overdue reform to the Iranian legal code that offers greater protection for minorities finally passed in 2013. Under the new law, in cases of murder the law looks upon the life of an Iranian Muslim and that of his minority compatriot as equally valuable when it comes to financial restitution to the victim's family. But the new law only includes religious minorities recognized by the Constitution, so Zoroastrians, Jews, and Christians are covered—only the Bahá'í are not."[432] The International Business Times also reported that under President Rohani the persecution of religious minorities has been "ramped up". It is very clear that the Iranian governments considers the Baha'i Faith to be a political organisation that threatens the government of Iran. As a result the Baha'i community has been the victim of systematic government oppression and persecution. Anybody perceived to be in any way associated or a supporter of an organization that is an enemy of state is also at risk of government persecution.

Christians face similar persecution, as a report from the International Campaign for Human Rights in Iran: "Despite the Iranian government's assertions that it respects the rights of its recognized religious minorities, the Christian community in Iran faces systematic state persecution and discrimination."[433] Atheists, persons who have converted from Islam, are considered to have committed apostasy. There is systematic persecution of atheists/apostates in Iran.

Conversion to Christianity or the rejection of all religion by a Muslim is referred to as "apostasy" which is considered a serious crime in Sharia law, so serious that many believe it merits the death penalty. According to a report by the UK "Christians in Parliament" regarding the treatment of those accused of apostasy in Iran: 'Most Christians who have been detained report that they were threatened with the death penalty many times by interrogators and guards. The possibility remains that male Christians could be sentenced to death for apostasy: although apostasy is not encoded in Iran's laws, judges can invoke Article 167 of Iran's Constitution, which allows them to refer to 'authentic Islamic sources or authoritative Fatwas' when making their judgements. Under Sharia law, apostasy is punishable by death for men and life imprisonment for women."[434] Muslims who have rejected all religion face similar risks.

Likewise a special report on apostasy by the Iran Human Rights Documentation Center stated: 'Under Iranian law, a Muslim who leaves his or her faith or converts to another religion can be charged with apostasy. In addition, any person, Muslim or non-Muslim, may be charged with the crime of "swearing at the Prophet" if he or she makes utterances that are deemed derogatory towards the Prophet Mohammad, other Shi'a holy figures, or other divine prophets. Both apostasy and swearing at the Prophet are capital offences. While the latter has been specifically criminalized in the Islamic Penal Code, the former has not been explicitly mentioned as a crime. Nevertheless, provisions in the Islamic Penal Code and the Iranian Constitution state that Shari'a, or Islamic religious law, applies to situations in which the law is silent. As a result, the Iranian judiciary is empowered to bring apostasy charges based on its interpretation of Shari'a law."[435]

The March 2015 The Christians in Parliament report on 'The persecution of Christians in Iran' published in 2015 concluded: "The most severe abuse is faced by Christians who have converted from a Muslim background, and those who engage in ministry among Persian-speaking people of a Muslim background … 'Christian converts in Iran - and any Christians who minister among individuals from a Muslim background - know they are either already being monitored by the Ministry of Intelligence and Security (MOIS), or that MOIS may identify them and begin monitoring at any time."[436]

There is considerable evidence of ill treatment of Christians and in particular converts by the Iranian state, with some experiencing prolonged imprisonment and torture.[437]

Christians in Iran have also been increasingly subjected to arbitrary arrests and detentions and the rate of arrests, detentions and prosecutions is increasing. The duration of imprisonment varies and can last up to several years, but in many cases, Christians are additionally charged with crimes that enable the authorities to detain them for significant periods of time. According to the International Campaign for Human Rights in Iran: "Most Christians arrested by authorities are eventually released, often with heavy bails. However, in many cases the investigations are never closed, nor are charges, if there are any, dismissed. This enables the government to restrict the person's religious practice through the threat of future arrest or prosecution. Most publicly reported arrests have been attributed to the Ministry of Intelligence. However, starting in May of 2012 the Campaign began receiving reports from multiple sources of involvement by the Iranian Revolutionary Guard in arrests."[438]

According to a report by a Danish Immigration Service "Fact Finding Mission", apart from direct persecution by the state converts from Islam to Christianity face severe discrimination in Iran: "Converts would have to hide their faith in order to be employed in certain jobs. For many jobs it is necessary to fill out a form in which one's religion is indicated. Overall, there is widespread discrimination against minorities with regard to access to education and employment. The impact of discrimination may vary depending on whether an individual is employed in a private company or a government position. However, even in privately owned companies, employers may be forced by the authorities to dismiss employees on the grounds of their religious faith."[439]

According to a recent report by Amnesty International (AI), atheists are "at risk of persecution, including arrest, imprisonment and possible execution". [440] The 2015 ACCORD report stated that "atheism is not recognized in Iran and that under Iran's Sharia law, any Muslim who abandons his faith may face the death penalty for apostasy". [441]. According to the Economist, Sharia Law as practiced in Iran "assumes people are born into their parents' religion" and consequently "ex-Muslim atheists are guilty of apostasy – a hudud crime against God."[442] The International Religious Freedom Report for 2017 refers to the execution of 22 Sunni Muslims for "enmity against God" and the widespread use of this offence to arrest persons from minorities and perceived opponents of the regime.[443] It is very common for atheists in Muslim countries such as Pakistan or Iran to conceal their identity in order to avoid accusations of blasphemy or other difficulties with the authorities. The most obvious identifier are the observance of holy days and fasting periods, and it is common for non-believers to pretend to participate in the observance of Muslim holy days to avoid detection.

8.4 Surveillance of dissidents and suspects

The Islamic Republic of Iran possesses a technological and legislative arsenal that allows it to keep its Internet under close surveillance. Interception of mail, filtering, control of Internet Service Providers, prohibitions, and monitoring of email content, chats and VoIP conversations are all legal.

In October 2005 the Supreme Leader of Iran, Ayatollah Khamenei, instructed the Command Headquarters of the Armed Forces to identify any persons adhering to the Baha'i Faith and monitor all their activities as well gather all available information about the members of the Baha'i community. This instruction was contained in a letter sent to the Ministry of Information, the Police Force and the Revolutionary Guard.[444] The document was brought to international public attention by Asma Jahangir, Special Rapporteur of the United Nations Commission on Human Rights and freedom of religion or belief.

The Special Rapporteur expressed her concern about the treatment of members of the Baha'i community in Iran. According to the press release:

"The Special Rapporteur is apprehensive about the initiative to monitor the activities of individuals merely because they adhere to a religion that differs from the state religion. She considers that such monitoring constitutes an impermissible and unacceptable interference with the rights of members of religious minorities. She also expresses concern that the information gained as a result of such monitoring will be used as a basis for the increased persecution of, and discrimination against, members of the Bahá'í Faith, in violation of international standards. The Special Rapporteur on freedom of religion or belief has closely monitored the treatment of religious minorities in Iran, and has long been concerned by the systematic discrimination against members of the Bahá'í community. Since taking up the mandate in July 2004, the Special Rapporteur has intervened with the government on a number of occasions regarding the treatment of the Bahá'í community."[445]

Blogger, online activists and technical staff supporting websites have fallen foul of the regime and faced harassment, abuse and jail.[446] In 2006 and 2010 the organisation Reporters Without Border included Iran as belonging to a group of countries designated as "Enemies of the Internet.[447]

In advance of the March 2012 elections, the Iran government put in place strict rules on cybercafés. All Iranians are required to register their web sites with the Ministry of art and culture. At the beginning of March 2012, Iran's Supreme Leader Ayatollah Ali Khamenei, instructed Iranian authorities to create an institution to oversee the Internet called The Supreme Council of Virtual Space consisting of the president, culture and information minister, the police and Revolutionary Guard chiefs.[448].

Social media are considered to be a serious political threat and for this reason the regime has used filter technology to prevent access to them even though many people have been able to by-pass the filters using virtual private networks. The head of the Iranian police, Esmaeil Ahmadi Moghadam, proposed in January 2013 that the government was developing technology that for greater surveillance of social networks, especially Twitter and Facebook. The idea is to "avoid the evils of social networks" while "benefiting from their useful applications". Given that government officials are using social networks, there is a view that it would better to control them rather than banning them outright which is the prevailing policy.[449]

There is clear evidence that Facebook and other social network sites are used to trace the activities of private persons in a manner that can result in serious consequences for those concerned. For example, a 25-year-old Iranian said his Facebook activity has led to his father's detention in a notorious prison in Tehran. And now he's struggling to find a way to free him. "I want my family to forgive me," Yashar Khameneh said. "But I believe what I believe in." While studying at a college in Holland, Yashar Khameneh joined a Facebook page while studying in Holland that made fun of a top Shiite Muslim imam, Ali al-Naqi al-Hadi. Naqi is one of 12 imams considered successors to the Prophet Mohammed. Insulting him can result in arrest.[450]

The US State Department in its HR report for Iran of 2012 reported that —The [Iranian] government monitored Internet communications, especially social networking Web sites, such as Facebook, Twitter, and YouTube. Freedom House and other human rights organizations reported that authorities sometimes stopped citizens at Tehran International Airport as they arrived in the country, asked them to log into their YouTube and Facebook accounts, and in some cases forced them to delete information." According to a report on government activities observing overseas protests indicates that: "The Iran Report cites a July 2009 article in the Times expressing concern over filming of demonstrations outside the Iranian embassy in London (Iran 15.09)."[451] The objective evidence is unambiguously clear about the fact the Iranian government is using all the means of surveillance possible to observe dissenters. This includes all electronic means of communication as well as the interception of mail.

8.5 Treatment of returned asylum seekers in Iran

It is very difficult for outside analysts to trace people after they are returned to countries such as Iran, which is characterized by high levels of repression and human rights abuses. Iranian citizens who claim asylum abroad frequently have either engaged in political activities which are considered as a form of opposition and therefore illegal activity against the regime, and/or they are part of an ethnic minority that suffers oppression and discrimination in Iran. There criminal acts in the eyes of the regime involve leaving the country without permission, slandering the state by claiming asylum in another country, and their opposition to the Iranian regime. Iranian Refugees Action Network in regards to the return of ethnic activists to Iran states that 'There is no possibility of a safe return to Iran.'[452] Amnesty International in relation to this case states that: 'States are not permitted to return individuals to countries where they would be at risk of torture or other serious human rights violations.'[453]

In a report titled Stop *Deportation of Stockholm's Asylum-Seeking Kurds,* elsewhere the organization states that: 'The Iranian regime's new directives under Article 7 of the Iranian Penal code, namely the detention and prosecution of political refugees who return to Iran, mean that anyone who has applied for asylum on political grounds can be prosecuted.' The report adds: 'a European Court in Strasbourg ruled that Sweden's deportation of an Iranian was in violation of Article 3 of the European Convention on Human Rights.'[454]

According to Unrepresented Nations and Peoples Organizations: "four Ahwazi men, including the President of the Ahwazi Liberation Organisation, Mr. al-Mansuri. They are feared to face ill-treatment in an Iranian Prison. On November 30, Amnesty International issued the following statement on "Iran/Syria: Further information on Forcible return/Fear of torture and ill-treatment/ Possible Death Sentence." IRAN/SYRIA Faleh 'Abdullah al-Mansuri-Nikouseresht (m), aged 60, President of the Ahwazi Liberation Organisation (ALO), Dutch national Rasool Mezrea' (m), ALO member Taher 'Ali Mezrea' (m), aged 40Jamal 'Obeidawi (m), aged 34, student, Chair of Ahwazi Student Union in Syria. All four Iranian men named above are now believed to be held in Karoun Prison, in Ahvaz city in Khuzestan. One of them is known to have been previously sentenced to death, and all four are believed to be at risk of the death penalty, as well as torture and ill-treatment."[455]

The most prominent example has been extensively document by Amnesty International notes: "In February 2011, Rahim Rostami, a 19-year-old member of Iran's Kurdish minority who had arrived in Norway as an unaccompanied minor, and whose asylum claim had been rejected by the Norwegian authorities, was forcibly returned by

Norway to Iran where he was reportedly arrested. He is believed to still be detained, with bail reportedly having been denied. On 17 February 2011, an article written by a former Supreme Court judge appeared in Iran newspaper, a daily paper published by the Iranian government. Referring to existing laws that enable Iran's judiciary to bring charges against Iranians for alleged violations of Iranian law committed while outside Iran, the article stated that failed asylum-seekers could be prosecuted for making up accounts of alleged persecution. On 26 April 2011, Kayhan newspaper, which is controlled by the Office of the Supreme Leader, also reported that Iranians are seeking asylum 'on the pretext of supporting the opposition'." (Amnesty International (6 May 2011) Student Activists Held in Iran).[456]

A document in March 2011 released by Iran Human Rights states: "According to reports that reliable sources have given to Iran Human Rights (IHR), a Kurdish asylum seeker who was extradited from Norway to Iran on February 9th 2011, is in danger of torture and ill-treatment at Tehran's Evin prison." (Iran Human Rights (23 March 2011) A Kurdish asylum seeker extradited from Norway to Iran is in danger of torture and ill-treatment at Tehran's Evin prison).[457]

According to an Amnesty International Report entitled "We are ordered to crush you. Expanding repression of dissent in Iran", published in February 2012:

"Failed asylum seekers ... risk arrest if they return to Iran, particularly if forcibly returned, where their asylum application is known to the authorities. A report issued by a Swiss refugee agency quotes an unnamed judge as saying: 'Asylum seekers are interrogated on return, whether or not they have been political activists in Iran or abroad. If they have tried to conduct propaganda against Iran, then they are culpable and are detained until a judge decides the sentence. In recent years many people have tried to destroy the reputation of Iran and this must be stopped. Such people help the opposition groups and their culpability is plain. Returnees will therefore be held for a few days until it is clear to the police, that they have not been involved in political activity... If the person was either politically active in Iran before leaving, or has been active abroad, they must be tried and receive a punishment appropriate to their activities. This report followed an article written by a former Supreme Court judge which appeared in Iran newspaper, a daily paper published by the Iranian government, on 17 February 2011. Referring to existing laws that enable Iran's judiciary to bring charges against Iranians for alleged violations of Iranian law committed while outside Iran, the article stated that failed asylum-seekers could be prosecuted for making up accounts of alleged persecution. On 26 April 2011, Kayhan newspaper, which is controlled by the Office of the Supreme Leader, also reported that Iranians are seeking asylum —on the pretext of supporting the opposition."

In May 2011 an article in The Guardian reported: "Six Iranians who have been on hunger strike for 32 days in protest at plans to send them back to Tehran have held a demonstration outside the Home Office amid growing concern over their health." This article also noted: "The group's new lawyer, Hani Zubeidi, said their plight had been reported in several countries since the Guardian ran the story – including Iran. 'They would be in very real danger if they were return now simply because they have been featured criticising the regime even without the fact that they were involved in the anti-regime protests and were tortured.'[458]

On 6 May 2011, Amnesty International (AI) reported that Nineteen-year-old student activist Arash Fakhravar was reportedly arrested on arrival in Tehran after returning from France where he was an asylum-seeker. The circumstances of his departure from France are unclear. His current whereabouts are unknown, and he may have been subjected to enforced disappearance.' The AI report elaborated:

Mohammad Reza Fakhravar (known as Arash) was arrested on 31 December 2010 after participating in demonstrations against the authorities which took place in Iran in late December 2009 during the Ashoura religious commemorations. He was held for 30 days in solitary confinement. A family member told Amnesty International that on 19 January 2011, he was tried on charges of —insulting the Supreme Leader, and taking parts in riots and unrest. He was given a suspended prison sentence, which could be activated if he were to be convicted of having undertaken similar actions at any point over subsequent five years. In late January 2011, he fled Iran for Iraq where he registered with UNHCR as an asylum-seeker. He travelled to France on 29-30 January, where he was an asylum seeker In March and April 2011, Arash Fakhravar took part in demonstrations against the Iranian government in France.[459]

It is illegal to act against the country outside as well as inside and political offences committed abroad can be prosecuted if a person is returned to Iran. A forcibly returned asylum seeker is *prima facie* considered to be an enemy of the state/God and is subject to detention and the likelihood of very severe punishment that can include torture, mistreatment, lengthy periods of incarceration or even the death penalty. Iranian asylum seekers whom wish to return voluntarily to Iran amongst many documents they are obliged to sign a form which states their regret in applying asylum abroad.[460] There is consequently a severe risk for Iranian asylum seekers should they are returned to Iran.

The consequences of being returned as a failed asylum seeker was addressed in an appeal in the case between Elham Yazdani and the Secretary of State for the Home Department. In this case, which related to a person and her husband who had been involved with military matters, the appeals court judgement stated: "…the case has been approached on both sides on the assumption that they would visibly return as failed asylum seekers. The judge overlooked that there might, in this case, be a further difficulty with the authorities, sufficient to raise the case to the level of a real risk. That added ingredient brings in the element of suspected disloyalty, or imputed political opinion, which places the case within the Refugee Convention. There is therefore just enough not only to save the determination from being set aside for error of law, but to require a further finding in the appellant's favour."[461] It is common practice that persons returned as failed asylum seekers to Iran, if they are accepted at all, are interrogated and can be detained and subject to mistreatment and this is likely to apply to someone of military age who left the country illegally and who is implicated in what is deemed to be political activities against the regime.

It is clear that there are serious difficulties about removing an Iranian asylum seeker against his/her will. Thus the Australian Immigration Minister Chris Bowen asserted:

"The involuntary return of failed asylum-seekers can only occur with the agreement of the host country. And this can only commence after an exhaustive process of assessment and appeal, which can take years ... "Despite numerous attempts by Australia, the Iranian government has made it clear that it will not accept the involuntary return of failed asylum-seekers."[462] The UK government is not able to obtain emergency travel documents for Iranian asylum seekers who are refused.

It is the policy of the Iranian government not to accept Iranian asylum seekers who are returned against their will. As recently as March 2016, in the course of on-going unsuccessful negotiations between the Australian and the Iranian governments, the Iranian foreign minister Mohammed Javad Zarif stated categorically that his country would not accept Iranian citizens repatriated against their will.[463] There are still a significant number of Iranian asylum seekers whose case was refused but who cannot be returned to Iran.

CHAPTER 9

Conclusion

The study of the security and human rights situation in South Asia and the Middle East in some selected countries demonstrates some important key factors that affect persons who lived in those societies and who found it necessary to flee their home country for a variety of reasons. The first of these is the level of political and social violence that is something that those who entrusted with making decisions about whether or not to grant individuals protection have never themselves been exposed to. UK tribunals rely on the European Qualification Directive which defines the minimum conditions that must be met for a refugee to qualify for asylum. In terms of indiscriminate violent in a state, Article 15 (c) is relied upon which) "will only be engaged if the latter assessment discloses that the armed conflict is characterised by indiscriminate violence at such a high level that civilians as such face a real risk of serious harm" simply by being in a country. However, the judgement as to whether this condition is met remains a matter of interpretation. This study has not attempted to demonstrate this with respect to any geographical region, but has analysed the causes and nature of political and social violence in select regions. It is important to understand that the standards we take for granted in European studies do not apply, because we looking at areas where there is a surfeit of lethal weapons in public and private hands, where there is a high level of violence and political and personal disputes are commonly resolved with violence, where the rule of law does not function as it does in Western countries and where ordinary people often consider the police and law enforcement as a threat rather than a source of protection. We have studied geographical regions that would be far too dangerous for those who make decisions about whether or not to grant protection to visit themselves. It is therefore really hard for decision-makers to truly understand the risks facing those seeking asylum. For example, Karachi is one of the most dangerous cities in the world, and yet 19 million people live there. The fact that people live under very dangerous circumstances does not mean that the risk to individuals is not real. Many people survived the ordeal of the ISIS occupation of Mosul, and yet the entire population had to face the fact that there was a realistic change that any day might be the last day of their life. In other words, it is important to gain a true understanding of the risks that people in certain violence prone areas are facing on a daily basis, and what it would mean to return them to such an environment. Many refugees have experienced traumas that we in the security of the West cannot possibly imagine, but yet there is a risk that the process that they have to undergo when seeking protection ignores that and is itself deeply traumatic. The results of this study can be taken as the initial starting point of an understanding of the risks that refugees from selected regions of South Asia and the Middle East can face and the human rights problems that exist. There are specific issues in the experience and situation of each and every refugees that will need to be considered. But is important to develop an understanding of the country context to have an appreciation of why many individuals feel that they have to flee the country in which they were born and where they lived. There is a real question as to whether the asylum system as it is currently constituted lives up to the values of the protection of human rights that Western democracies profess.

SELECT BIBLIOGRAPHY

Amnesty International, Iraq: Evidence of war crimes by government-backed Shi'a militias, 14 October 2014

Amnesty International, Iraq 2016-2017

Life as an Atheist in an Islamic Republic", *Atheist Republic*, 6 March 2014

SHIA GENOCIDE: A CRISIS IN PAKISTAN Report Commissioned by: Lord Avebury – Vice-Chair, Parliamentary Human Rights Group (2014)

Sumatra Bose, *Kashmir: Roots of Conflict, Paths to Peace*, Harvard University Press 2005

Sarah Graham Brown, *Sanctioning Saddam: The Politics of Intervention in Iraq*, IB Tauris 1999

Buck, Christopher. "Islam and Minorities: The Case of the Bahá'ís". *Studies in Contemporary Islam* **5** (1): 83–106. 2003

Christians in Parliament, The persecution of Christians in Iran, March 2015

Heather Conley, Crossing Borders: How the Migration Crisis Transformed Europe's External Policy, CSIS, Washington DC, 2018

Iranian Kurdish Refugees in the Kurdistan Region of Iraq (KRI) *Report from Danish Immigration Service's fact-finding mission to Erbil, Suleimaniyah and Dohuk, KRI,* 2011

European Asylum Support Office, "Iraq – Security situation", 2019

SECURITY SITUATION IN BAGHDAD - THE SHIA MILITIAS 29 April 2015 Finnish Immigration Service Country Information Service Public theme report

Neha Ali Gauhar, *Honour Crimes in Pakistan: Unveiling Reality and Perception*, Community Appraisal & Motivation Programme (CAMP), 2014

Gosselin, Denise Kindschi (2009). *Heavy Hands: An Introduction to the Crime of Intimate and Family Violence* (4th ed.). Prentice Hall

Salam Hafez, *Crimes of the Community: Honour-based Violence in the UK* (London: Centre for Social Cohesion, 2008

Hussain Haqqani, *Between Mosque and Military*, Carnegie Endowment for International Peace 2005

Phelim Kine, "Pakistan's Shia Under Attack", *The Diplomat*, 5 July 2014

Topical Note Iraq: Baghdad - the security situation as of February 2015", Landinfo Country of Origin Information Centre

Landinfo, Country of Origin Information Report, "Northern Iraq, 2018

Anatol Lieven, *Pakistan – A Hard Country*, Allen Lane 2011

Niraj, Nathwani, The Purpose of Asylum, *International Journal of Refugee Law*, Volume 12, Issue 3, 1 July 2000, Pages 354–379

T.V.Paul (ed.), *The India-Pakistan Rivalry: An Enduring Conflict*, Cambridge University Press 2005

Victoria Schofield, *Kashmir in Conflict: India, Pakistan and the Unending War*, I.B. Tauris 2010

Adnan Sattar, The Laws of Honour Killing and Rape in Pakistan Current Status and Future Prospects, AAWZ Programme 2015

Ayesha Siddiqua, *Military Inc.: Inside Pakistan's Military Economy*, Pluto Press 2007

David Succhino, "Why the Iraqi Army Can't Fight Despite $25 billion in aid, training", LA Times, 3 November 2014

Relevant COI for Assessments on the Availability of an Internal Flight or Relocation Alternative (IFA/IRA) in Baghdad for Sunni Arabs from ISIS-Held Areas", UNHCR 2016

UNHCR, "The UNHCR Position on Returns to Iraq", 14 November 2016

Varun Vira and Anthony H. Cordesman, *Pakistan: Violence Vs. Stability – A National Net Assessment*, csis.org, 2011

ENDNOTES

1   Heather Conley, Crossing Borders: How the Migration Crisis Transformed Europe's External Policy, CSIS, Washington DC, 2018

2   Niraj, Nathwani, The Purpose of Asylum, *International Journal of Refugee Law*, Volume 12, Issue 3, 1 July 2000, Pages 354–379

3   Varun Vira and Anthony H. Cordesman, *Pakistan: Violence Vs. Stability – A National Net Assessment,* csis.org, 2011; for a more recent analysis see http://foreignpolicy.com/2017/01/24/pakistan-is-the-crisis-flying-under-the-radar-trump-nukes-taliban/

4   *Dawn News*, 3 April 2011

5   *Indian Express*, 30 June 2011

6   *Daily Times*, 26 June 2011

7   http://www.reuters.com/article/us-pakistan-militant-attacks-idUSKBN0LL0IS20150217

8   http://www.spokesman.com/stories/2017/feb/13/taliban-suicide-attack-targets-police-kills-11-in-/

9   http://www.satp.org/satporgtp/countries/pakistan/database/majorincidents.htm

10 Jayshree Bajoria, Shared Goals for Pakistan's Militants, Interview with General David H, Petraeus, Council on Foreign Relations, 6 May 2010, http://www.cfr.org/pakistan/shared-goals-pakistans-militants/p22064

11 Lahore 'was Pakistan Taleban op'". BBC News. March 31, 2009

12 Ahmad, Munir; Ravi Nessman, Ishtiaq Mahsud and Hussain Afzal (October 6, 2009). "Taliban claim responsibility for deadly UN blast". *Yahoo! News*. Associated Press

13   Khan, Riaz; Ishtiaq Mahsud, Babar Dogar (October 12, 2009). "Pakistan says 41 killed in market bombing". *Associated Press* (Yahoo! News

14   Based on very considerable personal experience of the author of this report

15   Ismail Khan, Dawn.com., http://www.dawn.com/wps/wcm/connect/dawn-content-

16   Reuters, 31 March 2009, http://changinguppakistan.wordpress.com/2009/03/31/beitullah-mehsud- claims-responsibility-for-manawan-police-attack/

17   Khan, Riaz; Ishtiaq Mahsud, Babar Dogar (October 12, 2009). "Pakistan says 41 killed in market bombing". *Associated Press* (Yahoo! News).

18   Zofeen Ebrahim, "IDPs from NWFP Revive 'Outsider' Fears in Karachi", *Interpress Service*, 8 June 2009; "Telling Taliban from IDPs a challenge for govt", *Dawn*, 17 May 2009

19   Jayshree Bajoria, *Pakistan's New Generation of Terrorists*, Council on Foreign Relations Backgrounder, 7 October 2010

20   See Amnesty International Report 2010, The State of the World's Human Rights, Section on Pakistan (p.250)

21   *The Tribune*, 21 June 2011

22   http://www.independent.co.uk/news/world/asia/pakistan-bombing-terror-attacks-lahore-explosion-isis-shrine-taliban-court-latest-casualties-a7594731.html (23 February 2017)

23   http://www.telegraph.co.uk/news/worldnews/asia/pakistan/11501836/Czech-women-kidnapped-in-Pakistan-freed-after-2-years.html; BBC News "Taliban's brisk trade of kidnapping in Karachi", 23 March 2012; http://mirpur.tv/kidnapped-uk-pakistani-recovered-safely-mirpur-tv-mirpur-news/ (8 May 2017); "Kidnappings of British Asians rising in Pakistan"
By Adrian Goldberg, BBC News, 2 December 2011
http://www.telegraph.co.uk/news/worldnews/asia/pakistan/9538637/British-woman-feared-kidnapped-in-Pakistan.html

24   *Election 2013: Violence Against Political Parties, Candidates and Voters*, Pak Institute for Peace Studies, 2013

25   https://www.cfr.org/interactives/global-conflict-tracker#!/conflict/islamist-militancy-in-pakistan

26 http://www.satp.org/satporgtp/countries/pakistan/database/
    majorincidents.htm

27 Varun Vira and Anthony H. Cordesman, *Pakistan: Violence
    Vs. Stability – A National Net Assessment,* csis.org, 2011; for a
    more recent analysis see http://foreignpolicy.com/2017/01/24/
    pakistan-is-the-crisis-flying-under-the-radar-trump-nukes-taliban/

28 Anatol Lieven, *Pakistan – A Hard Country*, Allen Lane 2011
    (Kindle edition used), Chapter 6

29 Lieven, op.cit. (note 3); for a more recent report on this
    phenomenon see https://blogs.tribune.com.pk/story/45886/the-
    curse-of-nepotism-and-kinship-in-pakistan/ (8 February 2017)

30 "Incidents of Political Violence Increased in January to March
    Quarter", *OnePakistan*, 31 July 2012

31 Daud Khattak, Charles Recknagel, "What's Really Behind The
    Violence In Karachi?", globalsecurity.org, 22 July 2011; "Karachi's
    Deadly Political and Sectarian Warfare Threatens the Stability of
    Pakistan's Commercial Capital", Jamestown Terrorism Monitor,
    20 April 2012; "PPP behind Karachi violence, not MQM: Arbab
    Ghulam Rahim", *The Tribune*, 23 May 2012; https://www.
    theguardian.com/world/2016/sep/26/pakistan-police-accused-of-
    illegally-killing-hundreds-of-suspects-a-year

32 *News International*, 10 May 2013

33 "Election Violence: PLM-Q Worker Shot Dead", *Express Tribune*,
    2 May 2013

34 https://www.pakistanileaders.com.pk/news/news-and-events/
    anp-chief-leaves-country-owing-to-perceived-threats-to-life

35 https://www.theguardian.com/world/2013/apr/14/pakistani-
    taliban-target-anp-leaders

36 https://www.ndtv.com/world-news/bomb-near-pakistan-
    politicians-house-wounds-six-police-515949 (12 March 2013)

37 Tahir Ali, "ANP vs Extremism: (Un)fair game", The Friday Times,
    19 August 2016. http://www.news18.com/news/india/pakistan-
    awami-national-party-leader-killed-in-blast-602904.html

38 Asia Foundation, "Pakistan – State of Conflict and Violence, 2017

39 https://www.dawn.com/news/957995, 3 October

40 https://tribune.com.pk/story/108242/dr-farooq-a-light-the-
    obscurantists-put-out/ (24 January 2011)

41   http://www.satp.org/satporgtp/countries/pakistan/terroristoutfits/MQM_H.htm

42   U.S. Department of State (U.S. DOS). COUNTRY REPORTS ON HUMAN RIGHTS PRACTICES FOR 1998, "Pakistan" (Feb 1999), Jane's Information Group (Jane's). JANE'S WORLD INSURGENCY AND TERRORISM-17, "Muthida Qaumi Movement (MQM-A)" (14 Feb 2003)

43   Human Rights Watch (HRW). WORLD REPORT 1998, "Pakistan" (Dec 1997)

44   Jane's Information Group (Jane's). JANE'S WORLD INSURGENCY AND TERRORISM-17, "Muthida Qaumi Movement (MQM-A)" (14 Feb 2003

45   Amnesty International. HUMAN RIGHTS CRISIS IN KARACHI (1 Feb 1996, ASA 33/01/96)

46   U.S. Department of State. COUNTRY REPORTS ON HUMAN RIGHTS PRACTICES FOR 1990, "Pakistan" (Feb 1991)

47   U.S. Department of State. COUNTRY REPORTS ON HUMAN RIGHTS PRACTICES FOR 1991, "Pakistan" (Feb 1992)

48   Declan Walsh, "Attack on Journalist Starts Battle in the Pakistani Press", *The New York Times*, 26 April 2014

49   "Pakistani politics – Upsetting the Apple Cart", *The Economist*, 5 September 2015

50   http://www.satp.org/satporgtp/countries/pakistan/terroristoutfits/MQM_H.htm

51   " Militant wings of political parties involved in Karachi violence: DG Rangers", *Pakistan Today*, 28 August 2013

52   "Violence in Pakistan – Cold Shoulder for Sharif", *The Economist*, 28 September 2013

53   BBC News Asia, 15 March 2013

54   *Election 2013: Violence Against Political Parties, Candidates and Voters*, Pak Institute for Peace Studies, 2013

55   T.V.Paul (ed.), *The India-Pakistan Rivalry: An Enduring Conflict*, Cambridge University Press 2005; Hussain Haqqani, *Between Mosque and Military*, Carnegie Endowment for International Peace 2005; Ayesha Siddiqua, *Military Inc.: Inside Pakistan's Military Economy*, Pluto Press 2007

56 Sumatra Bose, *Kashmir: Roots of Conflict, Paths to Peace*, Harvard University Press 2005

57 Victoria Schofield, *Kashmir in Conflict: India, Pakistan and the Unending War*, I.B. Tauris 2010; Kashmir: The History and Legacy of the Indian Subcontinent's Most Disputed Territory (Charles River editors 2017)

58 Narender Seghal, "Pakistan's ISI and Kashmiri Militants", http://www.kashmir-information.com, 2001; "Musharraf admits Kashmir militants trained in Pakistan", BBC News, 5 October 2010; "Pakistan's ISI sponsors Kashmiri militant groups: FBI", DNA India, 21 July 2011; "Militants Kill 8 Soldiers in Kashmir", United Press International, 25 June 2013; http://www.sundayguardianlive.com/news/11551-isi-divides-kashmir-between-let-and-jaish (5 November 2015)

59 "Kashmir: Why India and Pakistan Fight over it", BBC News, 8 August 2019

60 https://www.aljazeera.com/news/2019/08/pakistan-parliament-convene-kashmir-crisis-190806065706666.html

61 https://www.nytimes.com/2019/08/07/world/asia/pakistan-kashmir-india.html

62 https://www.npr.org/2019/08/07/748957876/pakistan-warns-indias-move-to-end-kashmir-s-special-status-could-lead-to-war?t=1565365308481

63 The UKPNP is not included in the government list of political parties in Pakistan (http://www.ecp.gov.pk/). However, there is objective evidence of its existence as an organisation and is active in Pakistan. "UKPNP leader calls on UN to protect rights of people of Kashmir, Gilgit-Baltistan", *Asian News International*, 2 April 2015. Its lack of official status as a party is related to the fact that its members and the organisation is persecuted by the authorities.

64 http://www.business-standard.com/article/news-ani/ukpnp-protests-against-pak-atrocities-in-geneva-seeks-un-intervention-116091901163_1.html (19 September 2016)

65 Mumtaz Khan, *Pakistan's Kashmir Policy*, http://ukpnp.net/watan-dost.html#.html

66 This is based on personal knowledge of persons involved in political activities and persecuted by the authorities in this area.

67 *Hindustan Times*, 24 May 2006; Inter Press Service, 23 January 2006; Jamil Maqsood, "Sardar Shaukat Ali Kashmiri Chairman United Kashmir People's National Party visited Belgium", Indymedia, 26 November 2009

68 Eloi Rylan Kolos, *United Kashmir People's National Party*, Tract 2012; https://defence.pk/pdf/threads/human-rights-issues-in-gilgit-baltistan-ajk-raised-at-un-published-june-25-2015-by-admin.382632/

69 "The Kashmiri Fighters Who Lost their Cause", BBC News, 24 February 2011

70 Zafar Iqbal, 'The other face of ISI', Countercurrents, 28 January 2010; http://drshabirchoudhry.blogspot.co.uk/2009/12/protest-against-isi-in-muzaffarabad.html; "Pakistan's ISI admits to detentions without evidence", STRATRISKS, 21 January 2013

71 http://www.ahrchk.org/ruleoflawasia.net/news.php?id=AHRC-UAC-033-2017 (23 May 2017)

72 http://www.firstpost.com/world/pakistans-missing-activists-might-return-mangled-and-tortured-a-view-from-across-the-border-3205902.html (6 January 2017); https://www.thecipherbrief.com/pakistans-isi-the-true-deep-state (20 July 2017)

73 Frédéric Grare, Reforming the Intelligence Agencies in Pakistan's Transitional Democracy, Carnegie Endowment for International Peace, Washington DC, 2009

74 "PAKISTAN: Another Azad Kashmiri becomes the victim of ISI butchery", Asian Human Rights Commission, 23 May 2011; Maloy Krishna Dar, "An Itinerant's Journey through Pakistan Occupied Kashmir", ARSIPSO, 2016; http://defence.pk/threads/human-rights-issues-in-gilgit-baltistan-ajk-raised-at-un-published-june-25-2015-by-admin.38; the author also has personal knowledge of specific cases of persecution of UKPNP members by the ISI

75 http://nadeem-jknapnsf.blogspot.co.uk/2009_10_01_archive.html

76 Human Rights Commission Of Pakistan, January 2011. Revisiting Police Laws. Edited and compiled by Asad Jamal

77 http://nadeem-jknapnsf.blogspot.co.uk/2009_10_01_archive.html

78 Rohan Gurnaratna and Khuram Iqbal, *Pakistan – Terrorism Ground Zero*, Reaktion Books, London 2011

79 Ashley J. Tellis, *The Menace that is Lashka-e-Taiba*, Washington, DC, Carnegie Endowment 2012

80 Sebastian Rotella, *Pakistan and the Mumbai Attacks: The Untold Story*, ProPublica 2011

81 "Lashkar-e-Toiba – Army of the Pure", http://www.satp.org/satporgtp/countries/india/states/jandk/terrorist_outfits/lashkar_e_toiba.htm

82 Christine Fair, "Lashkar-e-Taiba Beyond Bin Laden: Enduring Challenges for the Region and the International Community." Testimony Prepared for the United States Senate Foreign Relations Committee' Hearing on "Al Qaeda, the Taliban, and Other Extremist Groups in Afghanistan and Pakistan." May 24,2011. www.foreign.senate.gov/imo/media/doc/Fair_Testimony.pdf; Ashley J. Tellis, *The Menace that is Lashka-e-Taiba*, Washington, DC, Carnegie Endowment 2012

83 http://web.stanford.edu/group/mappingmilitants/cgi-bin/groups/view/217; *United States Department of State, Country Reports on Terrorism 2016 - Foreign Terrorist Organizations*, published 19 July 2017; https://www.crisisgroup.org/asia/south-asia/bangladesh/295-countering-jihadist-militancy-bangladesh (28 Feb, 2018)

84 Amir Rana, *A to Z of Jehadi Organisations in Pakistan*, p.263

85 Amir Rana, *A to Z of Jehadi Organisations in Pakistan*, p.263

86 Rohan Gunaratna and Khuram Iqbal, *Pakistan – Terrorism Grounds Zero*, Reaktion Books 2011, p. 173

87 Rohan Gunaratna and Khuram Iqbal, *Pakistan – Terrorism Grounds Zero*, Reaktion Books 2011, p. 173

88 US Department of State, http://www.state.gov/j/ct/rls/crt/2011/195553.htm#huji, accessed 23 April 2013

89 South Asian Terrorist Portal, http://www.satp.org/satporgtp/countries/india/states/jandk/terrorist_outfits/HuJI.htm, 23 April 2013

90 Rohan Gunaratna and Khuram Iqbal, *Pakistan – Terrorism Grounds Zero*, Reaktion Books 2011, p. 175

91 'Significance of Qari Saifullah Akhtar's Arrest', *Daily Times*, (Lahore), 9 August 2004

92 Rohan Gunaratna and Khuram Iqbal, *Pakistan – Terrorism Grounds Zero*, Reaktion Books 2011, p. 176

93 'Qauri Saifullah's Arrest Shows No One Being Spared', *Daily Times* (Lahore), 9 August 2004

94 Office of the Coordinator for Counterterrorism (April 2006). "Country Reports on Terrorism 2005". United States Department of State; "Ilyas Kashmiri Killed in US Drone Strike, Confirms HuJi", *The Times of India*, 4 June 2004

95 http://www.stanford.edu/group/mappingmilitants/cgi-bin/groups/view/217#note8

96 Vahid Brown and Don Rassler, *Fountainhead of Jihad – The Haqqani Nexus 1973-2012*, Hurst&Company London 2013, p.110

97 "Hizb chief Syed Salahuddin warns Pakistan against withdrawing support on Kashmir". The Times of India, 8 June 2012

98 https://timesofindia.indiatimes.com/india/hizbul-wiped-out-jklf-before-dominating-valley-militancy/articleshow/60150213.cms (21 August 2017)

99 https://www.unafei.or.jp/publications/pdf/RS_No60/No60_12VE_Suddle.pdf

100 https://www.unafei.or.jp/publications/pdf/RS_No60/No60_12VE_Suddle.pdf

101 Human Rights Watch, '"This Crooked System", Police Abuse and Reform in Pakistan', (Summary) 25 September 2016; see also Home Office Country Policy and Information Note: Land Disputes (January 2017), 6.31

102 https://www.hrw.org/report/2016/09/26/crooked-system/police-abuse-and-reform-pakistan

103 According to anonymous interviews carried out among Pakistani people. Pakistanis who had come to the United Kingdom would express this opinion without exception. Pakistani people still in Pakistan asked over the telephone would refuse to discuss the subject out of fear. Interviews carried out on May 2018.

104 Crisis Group, Brussels/Kabul

105 Matthew Rosenberg, "Taliban Wages War on Police in Its new Front in Pakistan, *Wall Street Journal*, 28 May 2009

106 International Crisis Group, 2008, 'Reforming Pakistan's Police', Asia Report N°157, 14 July 2008, International Crisis Group,

Brussels/Kabul; for an update on the issues discussed see https://nation.com.pk/30-Sep-2017/police-reforms

107   Anatol Lieven, *Pakistan – A Hard Country*, Allen Lane 2011 (Kindle edition used, page numbers not available, ; citations can be located using search function)

108   "Corruption as the main issue in Pakistan in 2019, Financial Daily, 7 January 2019

109   Lieven, op.cit. (Kindle edition)

110   For details on this incident and to corroborate the general statements in this paragraph, see Rosenberg (note 17)

111   Based on experience from similar cases.

112   Jane's Information Group, Sentinel Country Risk Assessment for Pakistan, 3 July 2009, for a more recent analysis see https://www.hrw.org/report/2016/09/26/crooked-system/police-abuse-and-reform-pakistan;

113   Muzaffar Ali, "Police torture 92pc detained men, 8pc women: survey", *Daily Times* (Pakistan)

114   Muddassir Rizvi, "Torture is routine Pakistani police procedure", *Chowk*, 12 November 2009; for more recent accounts see https://www.pakistantoday.com.pk/2018/05/09/police-allegedly-torture-man-to-death/ and https://nation.com.pk/05-Feb-2018/police-allegedly-torture-23-year-old-man-to-death-in-rawalpindi

115   Philip Churm, "Reprieve aims to expose Pakistan police torture", BBC NEWS 2. July 2010, http://news.bbc.co.uk/1/hi/england/8783002.stm, accessed 10 October 2010

116   *Asian Human Rights Commission AHRC-SPR-001-2010 June 26, 2010* INTERNATIONAL DAY AGAINST TORTURE 2010 – PAKISTAN, p.3 This documents contains considerable evidence about police torture in Pakistan.

117   https://dailytimes.com.pk/187863/need-police-reforms/ (25 January 2018)

118   https://www.hrw.org/report/2016/09/26/crooked-system/police-abuse-and-reform-pakistan;

119   Anatol Lieven, *Pakistan – A Hard Country*, Allen Lane 2011 (Kindle edition used), Chapter 3

120   S.Raza Hassan, "Key Police Informer, family executed in Swat, *Dawn*, 27 October 2008; see also the account by Pervez Musharraf

how the suicide attackers from the attack of 25 December 2003 were tracked down through NADRA even though the information on the face of the ID cards was wrong, Pervez Musharraf, *In the Line of Fire*, New York, Free Press 2006, pp.249-50. This incident also shows that even terrorists consider it necessary to be registered with NADRA even if they alter the ID cards issued.

[121] See the official website, www.nadra.gov.pk

[122] Ray, Ashis (7 March 2011). "UK keeps eyes shut as ISI uses turf to hit India". *Times of India*

[123] Gardham, Duncan (19 July 2011). "Pakistani spies 'operating in Britain'". *The Telegraph.*

[124] "Pakistan is spying on its citizens, says report by British NGO", Scroll.in, 21 July 2015

[125] Umbreen Javaid, Tahmina Aslam, FEUDALISM IN PAKISTAN: MYTH OR REALITY/CHALLENGES TO FEUDALISm, http://pu.edu.pk/images/journal/history/PDF-FILES/15_54_1_17.pdf

[126] Jahanzaib Khan, Humaira Arif Dasti, Abdul Rasheed Khan, FEUDALISM IS A MAJOR OBSTACLE IN THE WAY OF SOCIAL MOBILITY IN PAKISTAN, J.R.S.P., Vol. 50, No. 1, 2013

[127] Umbreen Javaid, Tahmina Aslam, FEUDALISM IN PAKISTAN: MYTH OR REALITY/CHALLENGES TO FEUDALISM, http://pu.edu.pk/images/journal/history/PDF-FILES/15_54_1_17.pdf

[128] Shuja, Sharif (June 22, 2007). "The sources of Pakistan's insecurity". *Contemporary Review*. Nicolas Martin, Politics, Landlords and Islam in Pakistan, Routledge 2015

[129] https://www.nytimes.com/1990/12/08/opinion/l-pakistan-certainly-has-a-caste-system-224690.html

[130] https://www.nytimes.com/1990/12/08/opinion/l-pakistan-certainly-has-a-caste-system-224690.html

[131] https://edtimes.in/pakistans-caste-system-is-scarier-than-indias/ (October 29, 2017)

[132] IDSN briefing note · Pakistan 2014, "Caste-based discrimination in Pakistan

[133] USAID COUNTRY PROFILE, Property Rights & Resource Governance, Pakistan, USAID 2010; USAID ISSUE BRIEF, Land Tenure and Property Rights in Pakistan: Failure to Address LTPR Grievances May Foster Support for the Taliban, Property Rights and Resource Governance Briefing Paper 4

[134] Project Management Revenue, Board of Revenue, Government of Punjab, LRMIS Background

[135] "Land disputes behind most murders in Islamabad", *Dawn*, 16 March 2010

[136] "Land disputes behind most murders in Islamabad", *Dawn*, 16 March 2010

[137] "Separate incidents: Three killed over land dispute in Jamrud", *The Tribune*, 16 December 2013

[138] "Four killed over land dispute in Gujranwala", *The Nation*, 28 August 2013

[139] "Three guilty of Pakistan land dispute murder conspiracy", BBC News 13 April 2012

[140] Gosselin, Denise Kindschi (2009). *Heavy Hands: An Introduction to the Crime of Intimate and Family Violence* (4th ed.). Prentice Hall. p. 13; Hansar, Robert D. (2007). «Cross-Cultural Examination of Domestic Violence in China and Pakistan». In Nicky Ali Jackson. *Encyclopedia of Domestic Violence* (1st ed.). Routledge. p. 211; Ajmal, Umer Bin (25 April 2012). "Domestic violence"

[141] Anderson, Lisa (15 June 2011). "Trustlaw Poll: Afghanistan is most dangerous country for women"

[142] "Violence against Women in Pakistan: A Framework for Analysis", *Journal of the Pakistan Medical Association*, April 2008

[143] "'Honour Killings' and the Law in Pakistan" by Sohail Warraich in Chapter 4 of "Honour, Crimes, paradigms, and violence against women" By Sara Hossain, and Lynn Welchman, Zed Books (London, 2005,

[144] "'Honour Killings' and the Law in Pakistan" by Sohail Warraich in Chapter 4 of "Honour, Crimes, paradigms, and violence against women" By Sara Hossain, and Lynn Welchman, Zed Books (London, 2005,

[145] Amnesty International, *Honour Killings of Women and Girls*, 30 August 1999

[146] Neha Ali Gauhar, *Honour Crimes in Pakistan: Unveiling Reality and Perception*, Community Appraisal & Motivation Programme (CAMP), 2014, p.11

[147] "Pakistan to investigate 'honour killing' case". The National Newspaper, Abu Dhabi. http://www.thenational.ae/article/20081028/FOREIGN/662811008/1103/NEWS; "Pakistan rejects pro-women bill". *BBC News*. 2005-03-02. http://news.bbc.co.uk/2/hi/south_asia/4311055.stm

[148] "Three teenagers buried alive in 'honour killing'", *Irish Times*, 9 September 2008

[149] Dennis Lynch, "Three Pakistanis Slain In 'Honor Killings' For Marriage Decisions", *International Business Times*, 29 June 2014

[150] Mustafa Qadri, "Shocking: Surge of Honor Killings in Pakistan", Amnesty International, 2 July 2014; Azam Khan, "Ministry Figures: 933 killed for honor in two years", *The Express Tribune*, 9 February 2015

[151] http://www.dailymail.co.uk/news/article-3694345/Of-course-strangled-Arrested-brother-Pakistan-s-Kim-Kardashian-killed-refused-stop-provocative-Facebook-posts.html (17 July 2016)

[152] Anecdotal evidence, based on the author's personal involvement with such cases.

[153] "'Honour Killings' and the Law in Pakistan" by Sohail Warraich in Chapter 4 of "Honour, Crimes, paradigms, and violence against women" By Sara Hossain, and Lynn Welchman, Zed Books (London, 2005,

[154] Amnesty International, *Honour Killings of Women and Girls*, 30 August 1999; for more recent reports and analysis see https://www.hrw.org/world-report/2015/country-chapters/pakistan, Mustafa Qadri, "Shocking: Surge of Honor Killings in Pakistan", Amnesty International, 2 July 2014

[155] Neha Ali Gauhar, *Honour Crimes in Pakistan: Unveiling Reality and Perception*, Community Appraisal & Motivation Programme (CAMP), 2014, p.29

[156] DAWN, "Crimes of Honor", 14 November 2014

157 Adnan Sattar, The Laws of Honour Killing and Rape in Pakistan Current Status and Future Prospects, AAWZ Programme 2015, p.26 f.

158 Asia Society, Report by the Independent Commission on Pakistan Police Reform',

'Stabilizing Pakistan through Police Reform', July 2012, page 88; see also https://tribune.com.pk/story/1570134/6-structural-malady-violence-women/ (28 November 2017)

159 Bureau of Democracy, Human Rights and Labor, Country Report on Human Rights Practices 2016: Pakistan, published in 2017, section 6

160 Anatol Lieven, *Pakistan – A Hard Country*, Allen Lane 2011 (Kindle edition used), Chapter 3

161 https://tribune.com.pk/story/1099692/pakistans-jirgas-in-spotlight-after-brutal-honour-killing/ (9 May 1016)

162 IRIN, *How justice works in Pakistan's tribal areas and beyond* 20 February 2013

163 Martin Lau, "Twenty-Five Years of Hudood Ordinances – A Review", 64 WASH. & LEE L. REV. 1291 (2007)

164 "Hudood Ordinances – The Crime and Punishment for Zina", Amnesty International in Asia & Pacific, http://asiapacific.amnesty.org, accessed 19 October 2012

165 Muammad Munir, "Is Zina bil-Jabr a Hadd, Ta'zir or Syasa Offence? A Re-Appraisal of the Protection of Women Act, 2006 in Pakistan, *Yearbook of Islamic and Middle Eastern Law*, vol.14 (2009-2010), pp.95-115

166 *Protection of Women (Criminal Laws Amendment) Act, 2006, http://www.pakistani.org/pakistan/legislation/2006/wpb.html (accessed 19 October 2012); for analysis see Lau (note 1)*

167 See Lau (note 1), also "Women Protection Low Priority in PATA", *Dawn*, 25 April 2011

168 "Women's Protection Law Fails Rape Victims", *Daily Times*, 30 March 2008. This article cites a survey by the Aurat Foundation. For further examples, see PLJ 2010 Cr.C. (Lahore) 892, http://www.pljlawsite.com/html/PLJ2010CR892.htm PLJ 2009 Lahore 405, http://www.pljlawsite.com/html/PLJ2009L405.htm, (accessed 19 October 2012)

169 http://en.wikipedia.org/wiki/Federal_Shariat_Court_of_ Pakistan((accessed 19 October 2012)

170 *Daily Times*, 24 December 2010; the text of the judgement was provided to the expert and is included in the bundle

171 http://www.princeton.edu/~achaney/tmve/wiki100k/docs/ Adultery.html, accessed 5 January 2013

172 'Four executed for Adultery in Pakistan', *The Age*, 5 June 2007

173 Saheed Shah, "Pakistani Couple Face Death By Stoning for Adultery", *The Guardian*, 18 July 2010

174 Immigration and Refugee Board of Canada, *Pakistan: Circumstances under which single women could live alone*, 4 December 2007, PAK102656.E, available at: http://www.unhcr. org/refworld/docid/4784deeec.html

175 Shirkat Gah Women's Resource Centre. 4 December 2007, cited in the UNHCR Report (note 18 above)

176 Farhan Sarwar and Abdus Sattar Abbasi, "An In-Depth Analysis of Women's Labor Force Participation in Pakistan", Middle-East Journal of Scientific Research 15 (2): 208-215, 2013

177 http://www.unhcr.org/refworld/docid/4784deeec.html; see also Home Office, Country Information and Guidance, Pakistan: Women, updated 14 July 2014, that essentially confirms this assessment

178 http://www.causeofdeathwoman.com/the-womens-shelter

179 "New Pakistan law will likely worsen torture by police", *The Baltimore Sun*, 28 August 2014; http://www.causeofdeathwoman. com/the-womens-shelter; http://www.refworld.org/docid/ 4b7cee8528.html; http://www.casas.org.uk/papers/pdfpapers/ KAandothers.pdf

180 http://www.justice.gov/eoir/vll/country/canada_coi/pakistan/ PAK104261.E.pdf

181 http://www.casas.org.uk/papers/pdfpapers/KAandothers.pdf

182 https://sahsol.lums.edu.pk/law-journal/law-custody-children-pakistan-past-present-and-future

183 http://www.landinfo.no/asset/2942/1/2942_1.pdf

184 US Department of State, Country Reports on Human Rights Practices, Pakistan, 2014

185 http://www.dawn.com/news/969037

186 http://www.peshawarhighcourt.gov.pk/PHCCMS//judgments/
28-2013

187 Immigration and Refugee Board of Canada, 'Pakistan: Situation
of sexual minorities in Islamabad, Karachi and Lahore, including
treatment by society and authorities; state protection (2010-2013)'
[PAK104712.E], 13 January 2014

188 http://www.landinfo.no/asset/2942/1/2942_1.pdf

189 Pakistan: Incidents of violence or mistreatment involving sexual
minorities in Islamabad, Karachi and Lahore; loss of employment
or inability to rent housing due to sexual orientation (2014),
Immigration and Refugee Board of Canada, January 2015

190 M. Waqar Bhatti, "Sixty-year-old homosexual lynched by
vigilantes", The News, 1 November 2009

191 "Pakistan: Incidents of violence or mistreatment involving sexual
minorities in Islamabad, Karachi and Lahore; loss of employment
or inability to rent housing due to sexual orientation", Immigration
and Refugee Board of Canada 2015

192 Immigration and Refugee Board of Canada January 2014

193 Martin Lau, "Twenty-Five Years of Hudood Ordinances – A
Review", 64 WASH. & LEE L. REV. 1291 (2007)

194 Dr. Matthew Nelson: Review of the Country Information and
Guidance for Pakistan: Sexual Orientation and Gender Identity,
2015. http://icinspector.independent.gov.uk/wp-content/
uploads/2015/06/IAGCI-Review-CountryInformation-and-
Guidance-Pakistan-Sexual-Orientation-and-Gender-Identity.pdf

195 Based on interviews and correspondence by the IRBC with
representatives of the Neengar Society and the WEWA (Women
Employees Welfare Association), Pakistan: Incidents of violence
or mistreatment involving sexual minorities in Islamabad, Karachi
and Lahore; loss of employment or inability to rent housing due
to sexual orientation (2014), Immigration and Refugee Board of
Canada, January 2015

196 Freedom House. 2013. "Pakistan." *Freedom in the World 2013,
http://www.ecoi.net/local_link/268527/383095_en.html;*

197 https://www.buzzfeed.com/husseinkesvani/gay-muslims-in-
straight-marriages?utm_term=.cfqgZ3WAPq#.flRv9X4dYz;

[198] http://www.religioustolerance.org/rt_pakis.htm (accessed 19 May 2011); The Constitution, Pakistani.org (accessed 19 May 2011)

[199] https://www.opendoorsusa.org/christian-persecution/world-watch-list/pakistan/

[200] https://foreignpolicy.com/2016/05/16/is-pakistan-safe-for-christians/

[201] https://foreignpolicy.com/2016/05/16/is-pakistan-safe-for-christians/

[202] https://www.christianitytoday.com/news/2018/january/top-50-christian-persecution-open-doors-world-watch-list.html

[203] https://foreignpolicy.com/2016/05/16/is-pakistan-safe-for-christians/

[204] http://www.pakistani.org/pakistan/legislation/1860/actXLVof1860.html

[205] This is evident from the various examples cited in http://en.wikipedia.org/wiki/Blasphemy_law_in_Pakistan

[206] The US State Department reports how blasphemy laws are often used to settle personal scores – see http://www.state.gov/g/drl/rls/irf/2007/90233.htm; also "Blasphemy Laws and Intellectual Freedom in Pakistan", South Asian Voice, August 2002

[207] ANNUAL REPORT OF THE U.S. COMMISSION ON INTERNATIONAL RELIGIOUS FREEDOM, Washington, DC, 2014, pp.76-77

[208] Shamil Shams, Deutsche Welle 5 December 2014

[209] "Pakistan 'blasphemy lawyer' shot dead in Multan office", BBC News, 7 May 2014

[210] Shamil Shams, Deutsche Welle 5 December 2014

[211] Kazim, Hasnain (November 19, 2010). "Eine Ziege, ein Streit und ein Todesurteil [A goat, a fight and a death sentence]" (in German). *Der Spiegel*; Hussain, Waqar (November 11, 2010). "Christian Woman Sentenced to Death". Agence France-Presse. http://news.yahoo.com/s/afp/20101111/wl_sthasia_afp/pakistanunrestreligionchristian; Crilly, Rob; Sahi, Aoun (November 9, 2010). "Christian Woman sentenced to Death in Pakistan for blasphemy". *The Daily Telegraph*; Salman Taseer: Thousands mourn Pakistan governor" *BBC News* January 5, 2011 http://www.bbc.co.uk/news/world-south-asia-12116764

212 Barker, Memphis (31 October 2018). "Asia Bibi: Pakistan court overturns blasphemy death sentence: Christian woman to be freed after being sentenced in 2010, accused of insulting prophet Muhammad"; *Protests erupt in major cities as SC acquits Asia Bibi of blasphemy charges". The News International. 31 October 2018. Omer Farooq Khan (1 November 2018). "Pakistani Islamists are on the boil over acquittal of Asia Bibi". Times of India. Retrieved 1 November 2018.*

213 https://www.indcatholicnews.com/news/36028 (19 November 2019)

214 BUREAU OF DEMOCRACY, HUMAN RIGHTS, AND LABOR, 15 April 2011, http://www.state.gov/g/drl/rls/hrrpt/2010/sca/154485.htm

215 *Pakistan Christian Post*, 27 January 2009

216 Compass Direct News (20 May 2008). "PAKISTAN: DOCTOR JAILED ON 'BLASPHEMY' CHARGES :Police rescue Christian from angry mob". mychristianblood.blogspirit.com. http://mychristianblood.blogspirit.com/archive/2008/05/20/pakistan-doctor-jailed-on-%E2%80%98blasphemy-charges-police-rescue-c.html

217 Felix, Qaiser (10 May 2007). "84-year-old Christian accused of blasphemy to force him to sell land". AsiaNews.it. http://www.asianews.it/index.php?l=en&art=9226

218 "Man gets death sentence for blasphemy". Daily Times. 19 June 2008. http://www.dailytimes.com.pk/default.asp?page=2008%5C06%5C19%5Cstory_19-6-2008_pg7_7

219 "Murder of Christian Lawmaker: Can Pakistan Check Islamic Extremism", *Christian Science Monitor*, 2 March 2011

220 "Pakistani Police Allegedly Makes Threats after Murdering Christian", http://www.persecution.org/2011/01/19/pakistani-police-allegedly-make-threats/

221 "Pakistan student killed over 'blasphemy' on university campus", BBC News, 13 April 2017

222 http://www.christianitytoday.com/ct/topics/e/evangelicalism/

223 http://catholicexchange.com/what-the-catholic-church-teaches-on-evangelization; https://www.9marks.org/article/journalmust-every-christian-evangelize/; https://holyspiritactivism.com/2015/03/14/

why-all-christians-should-participate-in-street-evangelism/; http://matthiasmedia.com/briefing/2011/09/speech-and-salvation-1-are-all-christians-commanded-to-evangelise/

224 "A Conversation with Hadayat Din", The Christian Chronicle, July 2011

225 https://www.washingtonpost.com/world/asia_pacific/christians-come-under-threat-in-pakistan-no-one-accused-of-blasphemy-is-ever-safe/2018/03/15/d5f88f46-232b-11e8-946c-9420060cb7bd_story.html?utm_term=.65de1a474383

226 http://www.wnd.com/2013/03/muslim-mob-burns-christian-village-over-blasphemy/

227 http://www.express.co.uk/news/world/669921/Pakistan-Muslim-lynch-mob-chase-Christians-homes-demanding-convert-Facebook. 13 May 2016

228 All citations from: http://www.aljazeera.com/indepth/opinion/2016/04/neverending-plight-christians-pakistan-160406095729110.html

229 http://www.aljazeera.com/indepth/opinion/2016/04/neverending-plight-christians-pakistan-160406095729110.html

230 "Pakistani Police Charge 68 Lawyers with blasphemy over protest", *The Times of India*, 13 May 2014

231 "Cleric sentenced to death in Pak for blasphemy", *The Free Press Journal*, 1 February 2012

232 This was demonstrated in the murder of Punjabi governor Salman Taseer by a member of his security force for advocating a change to Pakistan's blasphemy laws, see "Taseer Murder Case", The Express Tribune, 1 October 2011

233 "Pakistan 'blasphemy lawyer' shot dead in Multan office", BBC NEWS 7 May 2014

234 S.Raza Hassan, "Key Police Informer, family executed in Swat, *Dawn*, 27 October 2008; see also the account by Pervez Musharraf how the suicide attackers from the attack of 25 December 2003 were tracked down through NADRA even though the information on the face of the ID cards was wrong, Pervez Musharraf, *In the Line of Fire*, New York, Free Press 2006, pp.249-50. This incident also shows that even terrorists consider it necessary to be registered with NADRA even if they alter the ID cards issued.

235 See the official website, www.nadra.gov.pk

236 This based on the author's experience in obtaining information from the NADRA database

237 https://www.indcatholicnews.com/news/36028 (19 November 2019)

238 "The cost of unbelief", *The Economist*, 15 December 2014;

239 BBC NEWS ASIAN, "What are Pakistan's blasphemy laws", 6 November 2014

240 This is evident from the various examples cited in http://en.wikipedia.org/wiki/Blasphemy_law_in_Pakistan

241 https://dailypakistan.com.pk/23-Mar-2017/547723

242 International Humanist and Ethical Union, Briefing on Blasphemy Crackdown in Pakistan 2017: Disappearances, Arrests, and "Blasphemy" Hysteria, 2017

243 https://tribune.com.pk/story/1363949/secularists-mend-ways-leave-country-says-pti-lawmaker/ (23 March 2017); https://dailytimes.com.pk/21232/in-the-name-of-god/ (25 March 2017)

244 There has been no actual Home Office Country Information and Policy Note on atheists in Pakistan, so the nearest applicable is Country information and guidance: Christians and Christian converts, Pakistan, May 2016

245 http://www.pakistanchristianpost.com/headlinenewsd.php?hnewsid=2819

246 "A Pakistani Atheist", *The Nation*, 14 March 2014

247 "Life as an Atheist in an Islamic Republic", *Atheist Republic*, 6 March 2014

248 Darshna Shoni, "Hate Crime Investigation into the threat against Ahmadi Muslims", 5 December 2010

249 Channel 4, 5 December 2010

250 All citations in this paragraph from "Hardliners call for deaths of Muslims in Surrey", The Independent, 21 October 2010

251 https://www.persecutionofahmadis.org/the-blasphemy-law-in-pakistan-ahmadis/

252 "Persecutions of Ahmadis", see note 11

253 C.Christine Fair, "Who is killing Pakistan's Shia and Why?", *War on the Rocks*, 20 May 2014

254 https://nation.com.pk/22-Feb-2016/shia-persecution-continues-to-spiral-in-pakistan-as-the-state-acquiesces-to-genocidal-violence

255 Abdul Nishapuri, Let Us Build Pakistan, "Shia Genocide Database: A detailed account of Shia killings in Pakistan from 1963 to 30 Aug 2014"

256 Phelim Kine, "Pakistan's Shia Under Attack", *The Diplomat*, 5 July 2014

257 See for example Murtaza Hussain, "Pakistan's Shia genocide", Al Jazeera 226 November 2012; Murtaza Haider, "Time for Shias to Leave Pakistan, Dawn, 17 February 2013; https://nation.com.pk/22-Feb-2016/shia-persecution-continues-to-spiral-in-pakistan-as-the-state-acquiesces-to-genocidal-violence; SHIA GENOCIDE: A CRISIS IN PAKISTAN Report Commissioned by: Lord Avebury – Vice-Chair, Parliamentary Human Rights Group (2014)

258 The HinduBusinessline," Unidentified gunmen kill 7 Shia Muslims in Pakistan's Punjab province", 7 September 2013

259 Mehr News Agency, Ishtiyaq Hussain Toori, "Shias of Parachinar victims of Takfiri terrorism govt-apathy", 22 April 2018

260 https://www.irishtimes.com/news/world/middle-east/at-least-19-killed-in-attack-on-shia-mosque-in-peshawar-pakistan-1.210 2804 (13 February 2015)

261 http://www.presstv.com/DetailFr/2017/06/28/526789/Pakistan-Shia-Muslims-Parachinar-Kurram-Agency-Taliban-Daesh

262 https://www.dawn.com/news/1341299 (23 June 2017)

263 https://www.pajhwok.com/en/2018/01/31/women-among-6-family-killed-parachinar-explosion; https://www.thenews.com.pk/print/275082-six-of-a-family-martyred-in-kurram-roadside-blast

264 Murtaza Hussain, "Pakistan's Shia genocide", Al Jazeera 26 November 2012

265 http://www.satp.org/satporgtp/countries/pakistan/database/Shias_killed_Pakistan.htm

266 https://nation.com.pk/22-Feb-2016/shia-persecution-continues-to-spiral-in-pakistan-as-the-state-acquiesces-to-genocidal-violence

267 SHIA GENOCIDE: A CRISIS IN PAKISTAN Report Commissioned by: Lord Avebury – Vice-Chair, Parliamentary Human Rights Group (2014)

268 https://nation.com.pk/22-Feb-2016/shia-persecution-continues-to-spiral-in-pakistan-as-the-state-acquiesces-to-genocidal-violence

269 Sputnik, Shia Militia violate human rights when fighting against IS: Researcher, 14 October 2014;Iraq crisis: Shia militia show of force raises tensions http://www.bbc.co.uk/news/world-middle-east-27953312

270 *Amnesty International, Iraq: Evidence of war crimes by government-backed Shi'a militias, 14 October 2014*

271 Belfast Telegraph. (5 January, 2018). Defence Secretary warns Isis dangers 'far from over'. Belfast Telegraph

272 Cited from Patrick Cockburn, "Iraq descends into anarchy: Shia militias 'abducting and killing Sunni civilians in revenge for Isis attacks', *The Independent*, 14 October 2014

273 2003: UN envoy dies in Baghdad bombing http://news.bbc.co.uk/onthisday/hi/dates/stories/august/19/newsid_3504000/3504255.stm *Iraq: UN convoy hit by explosion in Baghdad, mission reports.*
http://www.un.org/apps/news/story.asp?NewsID=49358#.VI4G0iusWSo
Bombings, shelling kill 20 in Baghdad Shiite areas.
http://news.yahoo.com/suicide-bombing-shelling-kill-14-baghdad-officials-185705106.html

274 "Islamic State Claims Baghdad Bombings", RFE/RL Report, 20 July 2014

275 Rheana Murray, "What life is like in Baghdad now", ABC NEWS, 13 June 2014

276 Rudaw. (13 January, 2018). Explosion targets convoy of head of Baghdad Provincial Council, kills 8

277 https://www.alaraby.co.uk/english/news/2018/5/2/seven-villagers-killed-in-suspected-is-attack-near-baghdad

278 https://www.alaraby.co.uk/english/news/2018/5/16/suicide-bomber-targets-baghdad-funeral

279 Attack on Police Station in Iraq Kills 9 People.
http://abcnews.go.com/International/wireStory/attack-police-station-iraq-kills-people-27423083
Attacks Kill 15 in Iraq as Country Battles IS

http://abcnews.go.com/International/wireStory/suicide-bomber-tanker-truck-kills-iraq-27494437

280 Car Bomb Attacks Kill 37 People in Iraq
http://abcnews.go.com/International/wireStory/car-bomb-attacks-kill-15-people-iraq-27364631
Iraq: 10 dead in attack on Baghdad Shias
http://www.alaraby.co.uk/english/news/583ec251-7e31-447e-be06-bf40d3baf2b4

281 Urgent – Car bomb explodes in Sadr city [11/13/2014]. For more recent such attacks, see https://www.aljazeera.com/news/2018/06/deadly-twin-blasts-hit-shia-mosque-baghdad-180606200819019.html; https://www.bbc.co.uk/news/world-middle-east-42686677 (15 January 2018)
http://www.iraqinews.com/iraq-war/urgent-car-bomb-explodes-in-sadr-city-2014-11-13/

282 Iraq Travel Warning, US Department of State.
http://travel.state.gov/content/passports/english/alertswarnings/iraq-travel-warning.html

283 Isis accused of ethnic cleansing as story of Shia prison massacre emergeshttp://www.theguardian.com/world/2014/aug/25/isis-ethnic-cleansing-shia-prisoners-iraq-mosulUN Reports Shocking Acts of Violence by IS Militants in Iraqhttp://www.voanews.com/content/un-shocking-violence-by-islamic-state-group-in-iraq/2470249.html
Iraq: Shia militias open fire at Sunni mosque, killing scores.http://www.telegraph.co.uk/news/worldnews/middleeast/iraq/11051283/Iraq-Shia-militias-open-fire-at-Sunni-mosque-killing-scores.html

284 https://www.gov.uk/foreign-travel-advice/iraq (accessed 8 May 2018)

285 "Advice for members on the deteriorating security situation in Iraq", SOS international, 14 June 2014

286 David Succhino, "Why the Iraqi Army Can't Fight Despite $25 billion in aid, training", LA Times, 3 November 2014

287 http://edition.cnn.com/2015/05/17/asia/isis-ramadi/; Dexter Filkins, "The Real Problem in Iraq, *The New Yorker*, 19 May 2015

288 http://www.independent.co.uk/news/world/middle-east/baghdad-attacks-market-blast-car-suicide-bombing-in-iraq-capital-isis-

victims-a7033436.html; http://www.independent.co.uk/news/world/middle-east/baghdad-bombings-isis-kills-more-than-100-people-in-24-hours-suicide-attacks-car-bombings-iraq-a7025866.html

289 http://www.dailymail.co.uk/news/article-3567130/Storming-barricades-Hundreds-Shia-protesters-invade-Baghdad-s-Green-Zone-tearing-blast-walls-breaking-Iraq-s-parliament.html; https://www.washingtonpost.com/world/protesters-storm-iraqi-parliament-in-baghdad/2016/04/30/0862fd3a-0ec1-11e6-8ab8-9ad050f76d7d_story.html

290 http://edition.cnn.com/2016/07/04/middleeast/baghdad-car-bombs/index.html; http://www.independent.co.uk/news/world/middle-east/isis-most-deadly-attack-weeks-one-world-probably-cares-about-least-a7118211.html

291 https://www.theguardian.com/world/2018/jan/15/suicide-attack-baghdad

292 https://www.alaraby.co.uk/english/news/2018/5/16/suicide-bomber-targets-baghdad-funeral

293 http://www.asylumlawdatabase.eu/en/case-law/uk-aa-v-secretary-state-home-department-2015-ukut-00544

294 "Relevant COI for Assessments on the Availability of an Internal Flight or Relocation Alternative (IFA/IRA) in Baghdad for Sunni Arabs from ISIS-Held Areas", UNHCR 2016; " Fear of Iraqi Sectarianism Fuel Sunni Exodus from Baghdad", *Financial Times*, 16 June 2014

295 *Mamouri, A. (2017). Shiite Kurds challenge Iraqi Kurdistan independence. Al-Monitor. https://www.al-monitor.com/pulse/originals/2017/07/kurdistan-independence-referandum-shiite-feyli-kurds.html,Salih, D. (28 September, 2017). The Kurds of Baghdad: What their Future Concerns? http://www.middle-east-online.com/english/?id=85096*

296 Salih, D. (28 September, 2017). The Kurds of Baghdad: What their Future Concerns? http://www.middle-east-online.com/english/?id=85096

297 Floray Drury, "List reveals which cities in the world you are most likely to be the victim of a terrorist attack: Baghdad is deemed the most dangerous on Earth… with Belfast and Paris Europe's two

deadliest", Mail Online, 21 May 2015; see also US Department of State, OSAC, Iraq Crime and Safety Report, Baghdad

298 http://www.migri.fi/download/61225_Security_Situation_in_Baghdad_-_The_Shia_Militias_29.4.2015.pdf?054bcf1525bfd288

299 "Death toll increases in Baghdad hotel blasts – Bombing undermines city's most secured buildings", The Kuwait Times, 5 January 2016

300 US Department of State, OSAC, IRAQ 2018 : Crime & Safety Report

301 Amanda Erickson, "Ten Years After the Iraq War: How has Baghdad Changed", City Lab, 8 March 2013; SECURITY SITUATION IN BAGHDAD - THE SHIA MILITIAS 29 April 2015 Finnish Immigration Service Country Information Service Public theme report

302 "Topical Note Iraq: Baghdad - the security situation as of February 2015", Landinfo Country of Origin Information Centre

303 https://www.washingtonpost.com/world/widespread-unrest-erupts-in-southern-iraq-amid-acute-shortages-of-water-electricity/2018/07/14/b9077b90-86c2-11e8-9e06-4db52ac42e05_story.html?utm_term=.7fbd91a98fa0

304 http://www.msf.org/en/article/iraq-there-lack-humanitarian-actors-baghdad-area; 10 June 2016

305 https://www.npr.org/templates/story/story.php?storyId=5394090; https://www.alaraby.co.uk/english/indepth/2018/5/10/iraq-as-parties-fracture-signs-of-change-emerge

306 http://www.aljazeera.net/news/reportsandinterviews/2014/8/23

307 http://www.al-monitor.com/pulse/security/2013/09/iraq-sectarian-displacement-basra.html

308 http://www.bbc.co.uk/news/world-middle-east-35607179 (18 February 2016)

309 https://www.hrw.org/news/2016/01/31/iraq-possible-war-crimes-shia-militia

310 http://www.rudaw.net/english/middleeast/iraq/19012018; US Department of State, Iraq 2018 Crime&Safety Report: Basrah

311 http://www.bbc.co.uk/newsworld-middle-east-20914273 (4 January 2013)

312 "Stop Forcible returns from Europe to Iraq", Amnesty International, 17 June 2010

313 Amnesty International, Iraq 2016-2017

314 https://www.alaraby.co.uk/english/Comment/2017/8/4/After-Mosul-Iran-backed-militias-will-ensure-sectarian-violence-endures

315 UNHCR, "The UNHCR Position on Returns to Iraq", 14 November 2016

316 https://www.nytimes.com/2017/09/26/world/middleeast/iraq-kurds-independence.html?_r=0

317 https://www.haaretz.com/middle-east-news/iraq/.premium-1.818744 (25 October 2017)

318 UNHCR Iraq - Mosul weekly protection update (21 October 2017)

319 UNHCR Iraq - Mosul weekly protection update (17 October 2017)

320 UNHCR Iraq - Mosul weekly protection update (21 October 2017)

321 https://www.amnesty.org/en/latest/news/2017/10/iraq-fresh-evidence-that-tens-of-thousands-forced-to-flee-tuz-khurmatu-amid-indiscriminate-attacks-lootings-and-arson/

322 https://www.theguardian.com/world/2017/oct/22/kurds-bitter-defeat-iraq-reclaims-kirkuk
https://www.thenational.ae/world/mena/us-congress-seeks-to-impose-sanctions-on-shiite-militias-in-iraq-1.674501
http://www.breitbart.com/national-security/2017/11/01/state-responds-to-iraqi-killings-of-journalists-more-voices-not-fewer/
http://www.aljazeera.com/news/2017/10/iraq-army-171031063012795.html
http://www.bbc.co.uk/news/world-middle-east-41641563
http://edition.cnn.com/2017/10/17/middleeast/kirkuk-falls-erbil-reaction/index.html
http://www.frontpagemag.com/fpm/265385/iran-shiite-militias-endangering-future-iraq-heshmat-alavi

323 Iraq 2018 Scenarios, Planning After Mosul, IRIS, Paris, July 2017

324 http://www.independent.co.uk/voices/iraq-isis-mosul-offensive-islamic-state-leaves-sectarian-infighting-a7525396.html

325 Amnesty International, 3 January, 2017

326   Human Rights Watch, 31 January, 2017

327   United Nations, 21 October, 2017; UNHCR, 2 November, 2017

328   UNHCR, 26 October, 2017.

329   Ensor, 19 October, 2017; Martel, 17 October, 2017

330   Al-Jazeera, 5 November, 2017; France 24, 5 November, 2017.

331   Mostafa, 23 October, 2017.

332   NRT, 10 November, 2017.

333   https://www.irishtimes.com/news/world/middle-east/kurdish-leaders-ask-for-world-s-help-as-100-000-flee-kirkuk-1.3262282 (19 October 2017

334   Kurdistan 24, 31 December 2017

335   Landinfo, Country of Origin Information Report, "Northern Iraq, 2018, p.16

336   Kurdistan 24, 25 January 2018

337   Kurdistan 24, 5 February 2018

338   https://www.al-monitor.com/pulse/originals/2018/01/turkey-iraq-is-isis-back-in-kirkuk.html

339   https://www.gov.uk/foreign-travel-advice/iraq

340   http://www.emro.who.int/irq/iraq-news/who-condemns-violence-on-health-workers-in-iraq.html (26 February 2019)

341   https://www.aa.com.tr/en/middle-east/iraq-4-killed-in-bomb-attacks-in-kirkuk-/1493699 (31 May 2019)

342   https://www.al-monitor.com/pulse/originals/2018/01/turkey-iraq-is-isis-back-in-kirkuk.html

343   European Asylum Support Office, "Iraq – Security situation", 2019, p.104

344   https://www.vox.com/2019/5/15/18624564/iran-iraq-embassy-withdraw-trump-attack

345   http://time.com/5506007/trump-isis-victory-islamic-state/ 18 January 2019

346   https://www.nbcnews.com/news/world/isis-still-acute-threat-u-s-interpol-chief-says-n966021 (1 February 2019)

347   http://fortune.com/2019/01/29/isis-remains-threat/

348   Landinfo, Country of Origin Information Report, "Northern Iraq, 2018, p.20

349   Kurdistan 24, "The threat from within: The Erbil attack exposes radicalization in Kurdistan", 25 July 2018

350 Department of State, Crime and Safety Report Erbil 2019

351 http://www.kurdistan24.net/en/news/7651292f-b7f8-40c7-9ca6-b001b63d7b34 (15 April 2019)

352 Kurdistan 24, "Villagers around Iraq's Khanaqin, Jalawla evacuate as ISIS attacks increase, 18 January 2019

353 https://www.csis.org/analysis/islamic-state-and-persistent-threat-extremism-iraq (30 November 018)

354 Landinfo, Country of Origin Information Report, "Northern Iraq, 2018, p.26

355 Sarah Graham Brown, *Sanctioning Saddam: The Politics of Intervention in Iraq*, IB Tauris 1999, p.217

356 Sarah Graham Brown, *Sanctioning Saddam: The Politics of Intervention in Iraq*, IB Tauris 1999, p.217

357 http://www.al-monitor.com/pulse/originals/2016/08/debaathification-iraq-kurdistan.html

358 http://www.al-monitor.com/pulse/originals/2016/08/debaathification-iraq-kurdistan.html

359 AAH (Iraqi Kurds – internal relocation) Iraq CG UKUT 00212 (IAC) §26

360 AAH (Iraqi Kurds – internal relocation) Iraq CG UKUT 00212 (IAC) §58

361 Home Office, Country Policy and Information Note Iraq: Internal relocation, civil documentation and returns, October 2018

362 Europe Asylum Support Office, Iraq – internal mobility, February 2019, p.20

363 Phyllis Chesler, "Worldwide Trends in Honor Killings", *Middle East Quarterly*, Spring 2010, Vol XVII, No.2, pp.3-11

364 Anecdotal evidence, based on the author's personal involvement with such cases; see also James Brandon and Salam Hafez, *Crimes of the Community: Honour-based Violence in the UK* (London: Centre for Social Cohesion, 2008), pp. 136-40

365 Amnesty International, *Honour Killings of Women and Girls*, 30 August 1999; "Three teenagers buried alive in 'honour killing'", *Irish Times*, 9 September 2008;

366 Tina Susman, "In Iraq a story of rape, shame and 'honor killing'", 20 March 2011, www.tinasusman.com; "Honor Killing – Iraqi

Girl Stoned", 29 September 2001,CNN Report http://www. youtube.com/watch?v=nfL8eEjHWsQ

367 Foreign and Commonwealth Office, Annual Report on Human Rights 2009, http://centralcontent.fco.gov.uk/resources/en/pdf/human-rights-reports/human-rights-report-2009

368 Landinfo, "Honour Killings in Iran", May 2009; Finnish Immigration Service, VIOLENCE AGAINST WOMEN AND HONOUR-RELATED VIOLENCE IN IRAN, 2015

369 Broken bodies, shattered minds: Torture and ill-treatment of women". Amnesty International. http://www.amnesty.org/en/library/info/ACT40/001/2001.

370 Danish Immigration Service, " Honour Crimes against Men in Kurdistan Region of Iraq (KRI) and the Availability of Protection", 2010, *www.newtodenmark.dk*

371 Landinfo, "Honour Killings in Iran", May 2009; Finnish Immigration Service, VIOLENCE AGAINST WOMEN AND HONOUR-RELATED VIOLENCE IN IRAN, 2015

372 Danish Immigration Service, op.cit.

373 Statistics from Iran are not available, and the Danish Immigration Service had to use more indirect methods to confirm their conclusion that honour killings are very prevalent in Iran. Landinfo, "Honour Killings in Iran", May 2009

374 John Leland and Namo Adullah, "A Killing Set Honor Above Love", *The New York Times*, 20 November 2010

375 "Revenge is important in Kurdish culture", *Irish Times*, 6 July 2004; " Iraqi forces killed 255 prisoners in revenge attacks, says rights group", Al Jazeera America, 12 July 2014; Freedom House Report Iraq 2016

376 Danish Refugee Council, *The Kurdistan Region of Iraq (KRI) Access, Possibility of Protection, Security and Humanitarian Situation*, 2016, p.45

377 Danish Refugee Council, *The Kurdistan Region of Iraq (KRI) Access, Possibility of Protection, Security and Humanitarian Situation*, 2016, p.47

378 Danish Refugee Council, *The Kurdistan Region of Iraq (KRI) Access, Possibility of Protection, Security and Humanitarian Situation*, 2016, p.47

379 Iran: New government fails to address dire human rights situation. http://www.amnesty.org/en/library/info/MDE13/010/2006. Accessed on 09/11/2010

380 Amnesty International. Iran: Election Contested, Repression Compounded. http://www.amnesty.org/en/library/info/ MDE13/123/2009. Accessed on 01/02/2011.

381 "UN: Hold Ahmadinejad Accountable for Iran Rights Crisis," Human Rights Watch, September 17, 2008, http://www.hrw.org /en/news/2008/09/17/un-hold-ahmadinejad-accountable-iran-rights-crisis

382 "Iran: Amnesty International Condemns New Wave of Executions," Iran Press Service, October 19, 2007, http://www. iran-press-service.com/ips/articles-2007/october-2007/iran-amnesty-international-condemns-new-wave-of-ex.shtml

383 Human Rights Violations And Torture in Iran Rampant as UN & Rights Groups Meet in Geneva. http://www.realite-eu.org/site/apps/ nlnet/content3.aspx?c=9dJBLLNkGiF&b=2315291&ct=8057393. Accessed on 01/02/2011.

384 Medical Foundation for the Care of Victims of Tortures. A year on from Iran's disputed election, Iranian torture survivors speak out. http://www.torturecare.org.uk/news/latest_news/3065. Accessed on 01/02/2011.

385 http://www.unhcr.org/refworld/country/IRN.html. Accessed on 01/02/2011

386 Refugee Review Tribunal Australia. 29 July 2009.

387 **Ashura** marks the martyrdom of Imam Hossein and is the most **important** date on the Shia Muslim calendar, particularly in Iran, where the vast majority of the people are Shia. It is celebrated with religious theatre and somber parades, in which men self-flagellate, and animals are sacrificed

388 https://persian.iranhumanrights.org/1395/11/shahnaz-akmali-11955/

389 http://www.pezhvakeiran.com/maghaleh-42701.html

390 http://www.pezhvakeiran.com/maghaleh-42701.html

391 https://www.radiofarda.com/a/f7-victims-of-88-ashkan-sohrabi/25210167.html

392 https://www.radiofarda.com/a/f7-victims-of-88-sohrab-arabi/25362369.html

393 https://www.youtube.com/watch?v=Dt-UTAsVI2E

394 https://www.radiofarda.com/a/f7-victims-of-88-mostafa-ghanian/25241627.html

395 https://www.iranhumanrights.org/tag/kahrizak-detention-center/

396 https://www.radiofarda.com/a/f7-victims-of-88-mohsen-rouholamini/24970973.html

397 https://www.radiofarda.com/a/f7-victims-of-88-mostafa-kiarostami/26762490.html

398 https://www.radiofarda.com/a/f7-victims-of-88-kianoush-asa/25231055.html

399 http://www.pezhvakeiran.com/maghaleh-42701.html

400 Advice from a lawyer in Iran written in Iranian constitution

401 Advice from a lawyer in Iran written in Iranian constitution

402 Advice from a lawyer in Iran written in Iranian constitution

403 Advice from a lawyer in Iran written in Iranian constitution

404 Advice from a lawyer in Iran written in Iranian constitution

405 Advice from a lawyer in Iran written in Iranian constitution

406 Advice from a lawyer in Iran written in Iranian constitution

407 Advice from a lawyer in Iran written in Iranian constitution

408 http://www.bbc.com/persian/blog-viewpoints-42590280

409 https://www.theguardian.com/world/2013/may/17/green-movement-activists-iran-repression

410 https://www.theguardian.com/world/2010/jun/13/saeed-dehghan-iran-exile

411 https://www.kaleme.com/1395/03/27/klm-244766/

412 https://www.youtube.com/watch?v=p6DPH29GtCA; https://www.youtube.com/watch?v=wpH6DDfGq1w

413 Iranian Minorities Human Right Organisation. http://iranianminorityshumanright.blogspot.com/2008/10/imhro-exclusive-interview-with-habib.html. Accessed on 01/02/2011

414 Amnesty International Report. PUBLIC AI Index: MDE 13/147/2008 **10 October 2008.**

415 Amnesty International. http://www.iranfocus.com/en/index.php?option=com_content&view=article&id=63

95:amnesty-fears-torture-of-arab-children-detained-in-iran&catid=5:human-rights&Itemid=27. Accessed on 01/02/2011

416 http://www.unhcr.org/refworld/publisher,HRW,,IRN,47f0c4b61a,0.html. Accessed on 01/02/2011

417 http://www.unhcr.org/refworld/country/IRN.html. Accessed on 01/02/2011

418 https://www.unhcr.org/uk/news/latest/2002/7/3d343a8a4/first-iranian-refugees-iraq-home-under-unhcr-auspices.html

419 UNHCR, *Iraq: Iranian Kurds to be transferred from insecure Al Tash camp*, 11. October 2005, http://www.unhcr.org/print/434b8e9920.html; UNHCR, *Iranian refugees flee Al Tash camp*, 8. July 2003, and Human Rights Watch, *Flight From Iraq*, 9 May 2003, http://www.hrw.org/en/reports/2003/05/09/flight-iraq-0

420 Iranian Kurdish Refugees in the Kurdistan Region of Iraq (KRI) *Report from Danish Immigration Service's fact-finding mission to Erbil, Suleimaniyah and Dohuk, KRI*, 2011

421 Iranian Kurdish Refugees in the Kurdistan Region of Iraq (KRI) *Report from Danish Immigration Service's fact-finding mission to Erbil, Suleimaniyah and Dohuk, KRI*

422 Department of Foreign Relations, Kurdistan Regional Government, "Citizenship", 1 August 2019; https://blogs.lse.ac.uk/mec/2019/07/03/minorities-displacement-and-citizenship-in-northern-iraq/

423 Iranian Kurdish Refugees in the Kurdistan Region of Iraq (KRI) *Report from Danish Immigration Service's fact-finding mission to Erbil, Suleimaniyah and Dohuk, KRI*, 2011, p.8

424 https://www.bic.org/media/Current-situation-Bahais-in-Iran

425 Friedrich W. Affolter, War Crimes, Genocide, & Crimes against Humanity Volume 1, no. 1 (Jan, 2005): 75-114 The Specter of Ideological Genocide: The Bahá'ís of Iran

426 Abrahamian, Ervand (1993). *Khomeinism: Essays on the Islamic Republic*. Berkeley, CA: University of California Press.

427 Buck, Christopher (2003). "Islam and Minorities: The Case of the Bahá'ís". *Studies in Contemporary Islam* **5** (1): 83–106.

428 UN Doc. E/CN.4/1993/41, Commission on Human Rights, 49th session, 28 January 1993, Final report on the situation of human

rights in the Islamic Republic of Iran by the Special Representative of the Commission on Human Rights, Mr. Reynaldo Galindo Pohl, paragraph 310.

429 Iran Human Rights Documentation Center (2008-05-14). "IHRDC Condemns the Arrest of Leading Bahá'ís". Iran Human Rights Documentation Center.

430 Lora Moftah, "Iran Religious Persecution: Baha'i Faith Leaders Remain Imprisoned After Seven Years", International Business Times, 15 May 2015

431 https://www.bic.org/media/Current-situation-Bahais-in-Iran

432 Elliott Abrams, "A Sad Anniversary as Iran's Brutalization of the Baha'i Continues", Council on Foreign Relations blog, 29 May 2015

433 https://www.iranhumanrights.org/wp-content/uploads/Christians_report_Final_for-web.pdf

434 Christians in Parliament, The persecution of Christians in Iran, March 2015; see also Home Office Country Information Guidance, Iran-Christians and Christian Converts, December 2015

435 http://www.iranhrdc.org/english/publications/reports/1000000512-apostasy-in-the-islamic-republic-of-iran.html (published 2014

436 Christians in Parliament, The persecution of Christians in Iran, March 2015;

437 U.S. Commission on International Religious Freedom, Annual Report 2015: Iran, 1 May 2015; see also http://www.opendoorsuk.org/persecution/worldwatch/iran.php

438 https://www.iranhumanrights.org/wp-content/uploads/Christians_report_Final_for-web.pdf

439 Danish Immigration Service – Update on the Situation for Christian Converts in Iran – June 2014 (www.nyidanmark.dk); see also http://www.dw.com/en/what-its-like-to-be-a-christian-in-iran/a-19002952

440 Amnesty International Iran 2017/2018

441 Austrian Centre for Country of Origin and Asylum Research and Documentation (ACCORD). September 2015. Iran: Freedom of Religion; Treatment of Religious and Ethnic Minorities, p.51

442 The Economist 24 Nov. 2012

[443] United States Commission on International Religious Freedom, 2017 Annual Report, Iran

[444] Esfandiari, Golnaz (2006-03-30). "Iran: UN, U.S. Concerned Over Situation Of Baha'is". globalsecurity.org.

[445] Jahangir, Asma (2006-03-20). "Special Rapporteur on Freedom of Religion of Belief concerned about treatment of followers of Bahá'í Faith in Iran". Office of the United Nations High Commissioner for Human Rights.

[446] Amnesty International. (2004.) "Iran: Civil society activists and human rights defenders under attack". *AmnestyInternational.org.* Reporters Without Borders. (2005.) "Reporters Without Borders welcomes release of blogger Arash Sigarchi" *RSF.com.*

Amnesty International. (2004.) "Iran: Civil society activists and human rights defenders under attack".*AmnestyInternational.org.* Reporters Without Borders. (2005.) "Reporters Without Borders welcomes release of blogger Arash Sigarchi" *RSF.com.*

[447] Reporters Without Borders. (2010). "Web 2.0 versus Control 2.0 - The Enemies of the Internet 2010".

[448] BBC News Middle East (7 March 2012). "Iran's Supreme Leader sets up body to oversee internet"

[449] http://www.dw.de/intelligent-software-set-to-control-social-media/a-16507868

[450] Ashley Fantz, "Son: Iranian Dad Arrested for my facebook posts", CNN, 15 July 2012

[451] Michael Collyer and Dulani Kulasinghe. Review of information on return conditions of origin for asylum seekers in the UK Report prepared for the Independent Advisory Group on Country Information. Page 29.

[452] Iranian Refugees Action Network. Ahwazi Refugees At Risk in Iraq. Accessed on 02/11/2013. http://iranian-refugees.org/2012/03/17/ahwazi-refugees-at-risk-in-iraq/

[453] Amnesty International Report: Iraq urged to stop deportation of Iranian Ahwazi refugees. Accessed on 03/11/2015. http://www.amnesty.org/en/news-and-updates/iraq-urged-stop-deportation-iranian-ahwazi-refugees-2011-01-14.

[454] Iranian Refugees Action Network. *Deportation of Stockholm's Asylum-Seeking Kurds.* Accessed on 02/11/2013. http://iranian-

455 refugees.org/2011/10/09/stop-deportation-of-stockholms-asylum-seeking-kurds/

455 Ahwazi: Syria Returns Refugees to Iran, accessed on 03/11/2013. http://www.unpo.org/article/5961

456 Accessed on 30/10/2013. *Amnesty International.* http://www.amnesty.org/ar/library/asset/MDE13/047/2011/en/2c6e1269-1974-46b4-977b-80509f2248c5/mde130472011en.pdf

457 Accessed on 29/10/2013. *Iran Human Rights.* http://iranhr.net/spip.php?article2015

458 Accessed on 30/10/2013. *The Guardian.* http://www.theguardian.com/uk/2011/may/06/iranians-hunger-strike-protest-deportation

459 http://acmeofskill.com/2011/05/amnesty-international-seeks-urgent-action-on-shiva-and-fakhravar/

460 The Islamic Republic of Iran, Berlin Embassy. Accessed on 01/11/2013. http://www.iranembassy.de/fa /گذرنامه/کنسولی-بخش/ عبور-برگ-صدور-227/گذرنامه-به-مربوط-امور

461 Upper Tribunal (Immigration and Asylum Chamber) Appeal Number: AA/04684/2013, UPPER TRIBUNAL JUDGE MACLEMAN, Between ELHAM YAZDANI THE SECRETARY OF STATE FOR THE HOME DEPARTMENT, paragraph 12

462 http://www.theaustralian.com.au/national-affairs/policy/iranian-aylum-seekers-caught-between-worlds/story-fn9hm1gu-1226242143934#sthash.whudC2Z1.dpuf

463 http://www.theguardian.com/australia-news/2016/mar/15/iran-refuses-to-take-back-asylum-seekers-who-have-been-forcibly-returned